RADICAL DISCIPLESHIP

CHRISTOPHER SUGDEN

Marshalls

To Dad

Marshalls Paperbacks
Marshall Morgan & Scott
3 Beggarwood Lane, Basingstoke, Hants RG23 7LP

Copyright © Christopher Sugden 1981
First published by Marshall Morgan & Scott 1981
Reprinted – Impression Number
2 3 4 5 6 – 86 85 84 83

British Library CIP data

Sugden, Christopher
  Radical discipleship. – (Marshalls paperbacks)
  1. Christian life
  1. Title
  248.4   BV4501.2

  ISBN: 0 551 00901 2

Biblical quotes are from the Good News Bible,
© American Bible Society, 1976.

Phototypeset by Input Typesetting Ltd., London
Printed in Great Britain by Hunt Barnard Printing Ltd.

Contents

Foreword

Radical discipleship means nothing more – and nothing less – than practising what we preach. It means living out the concrete implications of our most basic Christian confession: Jesus of Nazareth is truly Immanuel, God with us. It means surrendering every area of our lives – our security, our economics, even our politics – to the sovereign, unconditional Lordship of the Incarnate One who came and lived among us as the carpenter from Nazareth.

It is a stunning tragedy that those who insist most loudly on the full deity of Jesus Christ often fail most miserably to follow in the steps of the Master. Chris Sugden thinks that anomaly must end. And his book, *Radical Discipleship*, will help to see that it does.

In the last decades, an important movement determined to overcome the tragic dichotomy between evangelism and social concern has emerged in evangelical circles. Chris Sugden is a part of this new group of evangelical thinkers firmly committed to a balanced, holistic biblical approach. He stands solidly in the mainstream of historic Christian faith. But he has also listened carefully to Christians from the Two-thirds World where problems of poverty, injustice and oppression cannot be ignored. As a result, he is determined to combine prayer and action, building intimate Christian community and changing unjust social structures, evangelism and social action.

Radical Discipleship also reflects Chris Sugden's call to combine theory and practice. A well-trained British theologian, Chris lives with his wife Elaine, who is a medical doctor, and their two small children in a context of poverty, serving the church in India. The strength of his book derives from this combination of theological training and practical experience. There is solid theological reflection in *Radical Discipleship*. But there are also practical suggestions and numerous concrete illustrations drawn both from England and India.

Those concerned with radical discipleship rightly call for a new kind of partnership between the Christians in the First and Two-thirds World. Chris Sugden himself incarnates an exciting model of partnership in his unique collaboration with the influential evangelical Indian leader, Vinay Samuel, theologian and pastor of St. John's, Bangalore. Together, their work in development, their papers for international conferences, and their joint writings are making a significant impact on the world-wide church.

Radical Discipleship is not for the complacent. Do not read it if you prefer to remain undisturbed. But if, regardless of the cost, you want to follow our Risen Lord Jesus in the last two turbulent decades of the twentieth century, Chris Sugden's solid theology, practical suggestions and concrete illustrations will offer significant help.

Ronald J. Sider
Eastern Baptist Theological Seminary
January 13, 1981

Acknowledgements

My thanks are due to Michael Hews of the Scripture Union who had the idea for this book, and to Michael Eastman of the Frontier Youth Trust who has been its godfather. Mrs. Panchasheila Qadri, Miss Linda Kelly and Miss Noelene Marshall have typed the manuscript, and Paul and Pippa Julings of Aslancrafts Education Unit have helped in a number of ways. I am particularly indebted to my senior colleague, Rev Vinay Samuel and his wife Colleen. Over the two years in which this book was written it has been my privilege to discuss many of the issues in its pages with him as we collaborated in a joint writing team on many other projects. Inevitably in teamwork it is difficult and invidious to decide how ideas originated or were refined. Many of the ideas owe something to our teamwork. Finally, I would like to thank Ronald Sider, whose *Rich Christians in an Age of Hunger* has been a help to many of us, for writing the foreword.

Benediction

May the radical justice of God the Father, the liberating forgiveness of God the Son, and the revolutionary transforming presence of God the Holy Spirit, so blow through our lives that we may go forth into this broken world and fight the Lamb's war, knowing that the risen King has already won the victory over injustice, violence and death. Hallelujah! Amen.
Adapted from *Christ and Violence* by Ronald Sider, Lion 1980

Introduction

The 1960's and 1970's have witnessed an evangelical awakening to the social implications of Christian faith. The Festival of Light expressed concern about sex ethics, family life, abortion and pornography; Tear Fund has raised the issue of world poverty in Britain (and experienced exponential growth in its ten-years existence); Ron Sider's *Rich Christians in an Age of Hunger* has become a best-seller; *Third Way* started publication, as a magazine of evangelical social concern. The Shaftesbury Project initiated research and co-ordinated action groups on issues of social justice. 'Simple lifestyle' is discussed – and practised.

Workers among students, such as Rene Padilla and Samuel Escobar in Latin America, have incorporated social concern into their evangelistic and discipling methods. In the Philippines, the Institute for Studies in the Asian Church and Culture runs courses on development for evangelical students, as does Wheaton College, Illinois, USA. The House of the Gentle Bunyip, in Australia, is only one of many evangelical experiments in community living for discipleship and social involvement. Education for Justice is the latest of several activities of the Evangelical Fellowship of India Commission on Relief. In Nicaragua, Evangelical Relief Agencies joined a strike against the Samoza regime and participated in the resistance movement.

Social concern such as this was affirmed by the Lausanne Covenant of 1974, the text of which is reproduced as Appendix 2 in the present book.

We affirm that evangelism and socio-political involvement are both part of our Christian duty. For both are necessary expressions of our doctrines of God and man, our love for our neighbour and our obedience to Jesus Christ . . . We should share

God's concern for justice and reconciliation throughout human society and for the liberation of men from every kind of oppression. (From article 5).

But are these merely the preoccupations of a few enthusiasts, the necessary paper commitments of international gatherings? Many Christians, including pastors, church fellowship leaders, leaders of youth camps and mums' meetings, and of house groups, are perplexed as to the right relationship between such social concerns and the central Christian activities of evangelism, worship, and pastoral care. Is social involvement something which is only for the well-grounded believer – or is it part of discipleship right from the start?

Some of the groups and individuals mentioned in this book have taken tentative steps, and not a few risks, to show that involvement in the issues of how people relate to their society is a part of evangelism, discipleship, and Christian fulfilment. Their concerns find expression in the statement 'Radical Discipleship', drawn up at the Lausanne Congress, which called the Christian community to express the gospel in its life as the New Society, in its sacrificial service of others as a genuine expression of God's love, in its prophetic exposing and opposing of all demonic forces that deny the Lordship of Christ and keep men less than fully human; in its pursuit of real justice for all men; in its responsible and caring trusteeship of God's creation and its resources (for full text see appendix 1).

At the follow-up to the Lausanne Congress in Thailand 1980 one third of the participants signed a similar statement, which affirmed

evangelicals around the world [should] proclaim the gospel in word and deed 'in season and out of season' to all the unreached people. But they should do so bearing in mind that the overwhelming majority of them are the poor, the powerless and oppressed of the earth. The God of the gospel not only speaks (Hebrews 1:1) but sees the condition of the oppressed (Exod. 2:35) and hears their cry (Exod. 3:7, Jas. 5:1–5, Acts 7:34). Jesus himself set the example of an authentic evangelisation by proclaiming the gospel to the poor in word and deed (Matt.

11:4–6) . . . Evangelicals that lend their support to [apartheid, repressive governments, governmental denial of human rights, and the economic domination by the economic policies of developed nations and the activities of multinational corporations, over the poorest nations of the world] are a great scandal to the evangelical witness in general and to the evangelisation of the poor people of the earth in particular.

Nat Nkose of Scripture Union in South Africa, addressing the Thailand Consultation, spoke of his dilemma:

> I work among students who say 'You say that the gospel preaches love and unity of all those who have accepted Christ: but where is it demonstrated? We don't see it!' Evangelicals have failed to answer the challenge of these young people. Others who emphasise social concern are often weak in preaching the gospel. Both evangelicals and the World Council of Churches have failed to preach the whole gospel to the whole man.

Clifford Hill, the Evangelical Alliance's Secretary for Evangelism and Church Growth, wrote in *Third Way*, September 1980:

> The major barrier to the evangelisation of Britain lies within us, the Christians, the whole Body of Christ . . . We are sick because of our divisions, because of our narrow parochialism, because of our denominationalism, because of our lack of love . . . At a time when our nation is facing economic disaster, social disintegration, moral decay and spiritual apostasy, what is desperately needed is a prophetic witness from the church as the people of God . . . Why can't social action Christians burn with a passion to preach Christ as saviour? I certainly have walked that road and come to love the Scriptures as the authoritative word of God. My journey into new life in Christ began through a renewing experience in the Holy Spirit. Equally, why can't evangelical Christians burn with a zeal for social justice as the prophets did? Why can't they feel compassion for the poor, the unlovely and the outcast as Jesus did?

The concern to bring social justice and evangelism and discipleship together is worldwide, strong, and (according to Nkose and Hill) urgent. Who then are the groups attempting to do this? What are they learning? What are they seeking to share?

It has been my privilege to study and work with some of these groups; in particular in two very similar cities – Leeds in England and Bangalore in India. Both are industrial cities. Both contain the powerful and the powerless, the affluent and the poor; both have sizeable Christian churches among the middle classes and struggling congregations among poor communities. St George's, Leeds, where I worked, is a middle-class church which has a nation-wide reputation for its work among homeless men (which celebrated its jubilee in 1980); St John's, Bangalore, where I now work, is a middle-class church which has developed ministries among old people, refugees, slum children, and prostitutes.

In these pages, I offer an explanation of the concerns of radical discipleship, the experiences of some groups in discipleship training, and a guide to the reflections and insights on the Scriptures that they wish to share with other Christian. As I have read, and learned from, some of the writings of these groups, I have been struck by the fact that they are the first to deny that they have discovered any final answers. They have no blueprints, no ready-made solutions. They do not attempt to force on everybody the acceptance of dogmatic statements. Humbly they admit to inconsistencies, some uncertainty, a number of failures, on occasions even despair and doubt. But they have a fire in their bones which they cannot put out, and which keeps their feet on the pilgrimage they have begun. They do not demand that others copy or repeat their experiments. They seek, with us all, to be obedient to the vision that they believe the Spirit gives us in the Scriptures, and to follow Jesus.

1: New perspectives

Where do the scars come from?

One hundred years ago, science posed the major challenge to belief in God. But paradoxically, that very debate revealed to many people more of the wonders of God's creative power than they had previously grasped. Today, some Christians fear that sociology and social analysis threaten the significance of the individual before God; but these studies can possibly lead to a fuller understanding of the problem of man, evil, and the extent of God's deliverance from it.

The heart-aching contemporary question that challenges the justice and love of God concerns the poverty and dependence of two-thirds of the world's population. Why do one thousand million human beings, created and loved by God, live in extreme degradation? Robert Macnamara (until recently the President of the World Bank) describes the world situation:

> What are we to say to a world in which hundreds of millions of people are not poor in statistical terms but are faced with day-to-day deprivations that degrade human dignity to levels which no statistics can adequately describe? . . .a developing world in which there are more than 100,000,000 more illiterates than there were twenty years ago? A developing world, in short, in which death and disease are rampant, education and employment scarce, squalor and stagnation common and opportunity and realisation of personal potential drastically limited. This is the world today for the 2,000,000,000 human beings who live in more than 95 developing countries.[1]

Julius Nyerere analyses the problem in this way:

> The real problem of the modern world, the thing which creates

misery, wars and hatred amongst men, is the division of mankind into rich and poor . . . The reality and the depth of the problem arises because the man who is rich has power over the lives of those who are poor . . . Those who control a man's livelihood control a man. His freedom is eroded and his equal humanity is denied when he depends upon others for the right to work and the right to eat . . . Human dignity cannot be given to a man by the kindness of others; indeed it can be destroyed by the kindness which emanates from an action of charity. For human dignity involves equality, and freedom, and relations of mutual respect among men. Further, it depends upon responsibility and on a conscious participation in the life of the society in which man moves and works. The whole structure of national societies and of international society is therefore relevant to the development of the peoples. And there are few societies which can now be said to serve this purpose.[2]

Duarte Barreto particularises this picture for India.

India is therefore as much the reign of inequalities and injustices as it is of poverty and misery . . . Our country is divided between the rich and the poor. This is the real and the greatest problem . . . Gandhi had said that such a situation would not be tolerated a single day in free India. And we have tolerated it since the time of Independence! What is worse, we might not even be much aware of the depth of the injustices prevailing in our country . . . or we might not question them radically.[3]

Robert Holman, a social worker for the Church of England Children's Society, and formerly Professor of Social Administration at Bath University, points out[4] that the Child Poverty Action Group demonstrated that in 1974 in Britain 13,000,000 people – 25 per cent of the population – lived on incomes that were less than 40 per cent above the qualifying level for Supplementary Benefits. These were the elderly, the unemployed, the sick and disabled, the one-parent families, low-wage-earners and immigrant groups.

Such people could be described as 'poor', if we adopt the definition he quotes from P. Townsend: 'Individuals and families whose financial resources and/or other resources including their educational and occupational skills, the condition of their environment at home and at work and their material possessions fall seriously below those commanded by the average person or family in society may be said to be in poverty.'[5]

Roy Dorey[6] sees another form of poverty in the depersonalisation of people's lives in Britain, where many enjoy a high standard of living and low-cost consumer goods by accepting routine unfulfilling jobs, and constantly moving from one anonymous residential area to the next in pursuit of work or promotion.

The question 'Why?' leads not to God, but to man. Not to any individual, but to the way men have collectively resolved conflicting pressures in economic and political systems. But very often, men demand an answer from God. The biblical writers do not answer the question. But they give reasons for fighting suffering and injustice. In Exodus, Psalms, the prophets, and – supremely – in the person of Jesus, God is called the 'deliverer'. His people experience and express it: the life of the Christian community is to be the evidence that God is indeed the Deliverer.

God is renewing many Christian communities. The 'Renewal in the Spirit' movement is bringing with it a new warmth in worship, a new sense of commitment to the Body of believers, and a new appreciation of the ministry of each member of it to all the others. Many Christian groups are sharing work, home and income to discover and express togetherness in Christ. Churches in deprived areas are developing new forms of church life as they become intimately involved in local problems. The church is discovering that God wants it to be more than a propaganda machine; that he intends the quality of corporate Christian life to be a challenge and a sign of hope to society around it.

One Bible for the rich?

A new awareness of social forces, and a new experience of God's renewal, send us back to the Bible with new questions. Is there a theology of social evil? Can the church demonstrate a convincing alternative to the social patterns

3

that disfigure mankind? How should Christians exercise the Spirit's gifts and ministries in their life together?

A group of Christians working in Latin American shanty towns asks a sharp question of the Bible – 'What does this book say to people who cannot escape material, social and cultural poverty; who are imprisoned in a sub-human lifestyle by powerful financial and political forces?' The question opens new seams in a mine that scholars and theologians in Europe and America thought had been exhaustively explored. We now find that material poverty spoils God's purposes for his people; that God delivered slaves out of Egypt; that he gave detailed instructions for the prevention of impoverishment; that he is just, and champions those most likely to be exploited; that the gospel of the kingdom of God is good news to the poor, and that Jesus directed his disciples to give to them.

Perhaps the theologians of liberation overemphasise one aspect of the truth. But their question reveals God's bias to the poor and Jesus' social involvement. Did those other theologians disembody practical truth, and thereby make the Bible more comfortable for the rich and deprive the poor of their Guardian?

Pass it on!

If we are finding new dimensions to the Bible's message – how do we communicate them? 'Evangelism,' Canon Alan Neech has said, 'is so to present Jesus Christ that men may make an intelligent response to him.' Do we limit ourselves to communicating well-illustrated ideas to men's minds, by words, in conversation, sermons, radio messages, books? Or do we also make Jesus Christ flesh by action, compassion, emotion, and the life and worship of the community?

The witness of such as Mother Teresa and Martin Luther King speaks more powerfully than much writing or preaching. But we cannot trade on the witness of others. Our words must be given flesh by *our* action. Christians in India often point to the contributions Christians have made to medicine and education in the life of the nation. The hard question is: Which Christians? From where? How long ago?

And, where should our action be now? The *Tear Times* of Spring 1978 carried a headline: 'Nicaraguan Christians strike for justice.' Margaret Winfield reported that the Evangelical Committee for Development had decided to join a national strike in protest at the assassination of the leading critic of the oppressive government of the ruling Samoza family.

In whatever way we may define the relationship between evangelism and social action, the two are necessary if we are to pass on God's love. And we need drama, emotion, art, poetry and worship, if we are to communicate the full range of God's deliverance. If our message is only words, then we only communicate words – not praise, love, forgiveness, acceptance or peace. We are a community catering to people, not disembodied minds.

Persons in community

G. K. Chesterton's famous correspondence-stopper in the *Times* – 'Dear Sir: what's wrong with the world? Me.' – is not canonical Scripture. Yet it is often quoted to reduce the problems of society at large to the individual, to reduce all society's ills to individual rebellion against God. Who, we may ask, is the 'me'? By all accounts Chesterton was an eccentric and delightful individualist. But he was still his parents' son and wife's devoted husband, a member of the Roman Catholic Church and one of the most vigorous of its champions. Could he have been the same man without all these? His laconic message to readers of the *Times* does not represent the total biblical picture, as we shall demonstrate.

If we reduce all problems to individual sin; if we proclaim the death of Christ as the solution solely for individual sin, and send the redeemed individual back into the world as if he had the answers to all society's problems as well as his own – we undermine the strength of the biblical message. If we do so, we encourage arrogance or irrelevance in Christian people. We create a tension in those seeking to find Christian answers to many social problems when they find the individualistic formulation inadequate. Has the

Lord of the Universe nothing else to say? We impoverish the biblical pattern, which is of *redeemed people* in a *redeemed society*.

The focus of the Bible is on redeemed persons-in-community. We should emphasise the value of the *person*, in western society with its reduction of people to cogs in a machine and in eastern society that suppresses them beneath authoritarian hierarchy. We should emphasise the value of the *community*, in western society with its violation of the individual and in eastern society that equates community with conformity rather than diversity in unity. The biblical balance is a rich resource of theology and action amid the social pressures that mould people today.

So why write a book?

A number of questions arise out of these recent developments in understanding our world and God's purpose for his church. Can we develop an understanding of the biblical message that speaks to and illuminates the social and personal issues of today? How can we encourage new Christians to bring burning social issues to the Bible and find for themselves a relevant understanding of God and the world and apply it?

We need, first, to look at some practical examples of how Christians are answering these questions today with what they call 'radical discipleship'.

2: What is radical discipleship?

No easy answers

As God gives Christians new perspectives on the world, and new challenges to faith and practice, some are responding with forms of discipleship that seek to understand and apply New Testament patterns of obedience and community to today's social problems.

The groups to be described would be the first to deny that they have discovered final answers. Their obedience is a pilgrimage. They have no blueprints or ready-made solutions. Theirs are not trendy approaches to be copied unthinkingly. The very fact that these experiments work in their own situations should discourage us from making exactly the same experiment in different social conditions.

Rather, let us see them as voyagers of discovery – leaving well-worn paths which could become cul-de-sacs, and seeking to go where obedience to the Lord takes them. They show us what they mean by 'obedience', and they may stimulate us to strike out in a new direction too. But not necessarily in the same direction!

Shared resources

'This book contains the most vital challenge which faces the church today. It is one of the most searching and disquieting books I have ever read.' David Watson was talking about Ron Sider's *Rich Christians in an age of hunger*.[1]

Sider documents the fact that 'North Americans, Europeans, Russians and Japanese devour an incredibly unjust share of the world's available food' (p. 38). He develops the biblical evidence of positive Christian action on behalf of the poor and concludes:

> We live at one of the great turning points of history. The present division of the world's resources dare not continue. And it will not. Either courageous pioneers will persuade reluctant nations to share the good earth's bounty or we will enter an era of catastrophic conflict.
> Christians should be in the vanguard. The church of Jesus Christ is the most universal body in the world today. All we need to do is truly obey the One we rightly worship. But to obey will mean to follow. And he lives among the poor and oppressed, seeking justice for those in agony. In our time, following in his steps will mean simple personal lifestyles. It will mean transformed churches with a corporate lifestyle consistent with the worship of the God of the poor. It will mean costly commitment to structural change in secular society (p. 196).

Sider lists and suggests experiments: sharing resources on a personal level, such as buying second-hand, using libraries for books, taking care of and repairing possessions, keeping a car for a number of years; enjoying reading, talking, walking, hospitality, museums, parks and low cost entertainment; eating simply, joining a food co-operative, making dishwashing a family time rather than buying a dishwasher, sharing lawnmowers, sports equipment, books, car; organising a 'things closet' in the church for items used only occasionally (edger, clipper, beds for unexpected guests, camping equipment, ladder).

Shared community

Some groups share resources by living in the same households or in closely linked ones, sharing a common purse. Sider argues,

> Christian communes have a symbolic importance today out of all proportion to their numbers. They quietly question this society's affluence. And they offer a viable alternative. (p. 157)

Peter Berger, the sociologist, adds the following consideration of the way people learn:

Only in a counter-community of considerable strength does cognitive deviance have a chance to maintain itself . . . against the creeping doubt as to whether, after all, one may not be wrong and the majority right. To fulfil its function of providing social support for the deviant body of 'knowledge', the counter-community must provide a strong sense of solidarity among its members.[2]

At St Michael-le-Belfry, York, a household of eight adults and several children share the parsonage with the vicar's family. Three have salaries, which are shared by all to release all eight for church ministry. In this way, they seek to release more money and time for the Lord's work. In Iona, the Christian community adopts a lifestyle to reflect identification with the exploited and poor of industrial Glasgow.

In *Basic Communities*, David Clark surveys communities sharing houses and incomes who in some cases earn their living through agriculture or home industry. He concludes:

These experiments [are] important models of what could be, if only . . . At least something is happening and is observable. People are seen to exist in our times who do not go along with the norms of consumerism and affluence . . . seeds can grow, but no seed means barren land. Even where the small and the alternative are regarded as politically ineffective, the importance of these ventures in seeking to give a new dignity to man is recognised . . . Alternative technology and alternative modes of organisation in relation to work must in the end mean an alternative form of society. Many Christians . . . have at least made a courageous and determined beginning in practice if not just in theory.[3]

A growing number of books record such experiments. E. F. Schumacher's *Small is beautiful* gives a detailed picture of the Scott-Bader commonwealth where the workers have a large stake in capital, profits and decisions. Sider (p. 174) describes the Reba Fellowship, Evanston, Illinois, which began with three people in 1957 and today has over 150 members in a dozen households placing earnings in a common treasury. The central fund pays directly for larger expenses, like housing and transport; each month everybody receives a personal allowance. The food allowance is the same as that for persons on Welfare in Chicago. Household living requires 'fewer automobiles, washing machines, lawnmowers, BTU's of heat, electric lights, square feet of floor space, TV's, stereos, stoves and refrigerators.'[4] Money saved is released for the poor in the community and around the world.

Members of the Living Word Community, Philadelphia, practise a looser economic sharing without communal living. Members of house group fellowships raise interest-free mortgages and loans for one another (Sider, p. 168ff.) In England, the Pakistani community puts Christians to shame. While Christians bewail the lack of mortgage facilities to buy houses in the inner city, Pakistanis raise mortgages among themselves.

The former Director of The Shaftesbury Project in England, Patrick Dearnley, lamented that much Christian money is locked up in stocks, shares and business investment, when it could be financing Christian mission in the inner city by providing mortgages for Christians to buy homes there.

Healing community

Lifestyle and economics are not the only reasons for sharing community. Many household communities and other groups provide a therapeutic community for those scarred by life: expectant mothers, ex-drug addicts, the physically handicapped at L'Arche, the terminally ill at hospices, children and young people from Belfast at Corrymeela. The strain of sustaining community life and caring for others can be intolerable, as David Clark observes.[5] There is also a tension between the unconditional help that is offered, and type of help that points that person to salvation. Both must be offered, but how help is offered is vital; there must be a proper balance between directive and non-directive help. To maintain this balance the community needs to spend time together honestly examining its aims and methods. The pressures of busy caring over long periods may

10

crowd this out, and I have seen the sad results of this over a long time in a Christian caring organisation.

Charles Mellis, in *Committed Communities*,[6] identifies four contemporary movements which emphasise community in the context of missions: Operation Mobilisation, Youth with a Mission, Diliram Houses and Campus Fellowships. Community is achieved for short periods of time within these movements to express a deep commitment. Such movements are highly attractive for young Christians. However, Mellis stresses the need for order in commitment. Commitment to Christ is the *foundation* of community, mutual commitment *forms* the community, and community commitment is *given expression* in commitment to a task. That order of priority is crucial – steps two and three cannot be reversed except at the cost of producing an activism which subjects the relationships between those involved to severe strain, preventable only by a decision to revert priorities and nurture community. Many of us have seen the tragic results of a neglect of this order of priority among Christian workers.

The mutual support of a committed group is seen by Mellis as a major new resource for cross-cultural mission in place of the solitary missionary. The comment of a curate, working for three years in a Liverpool council estate, bears this out: 'What folly to place one "professional Christian" family in a housing estate and pretend it's mission. I'm paid to be a Christian, and am seen as a crank and a fool for not getting a better job and moving to a better area. But if a group of six Christian families moved here – our relationship together and with others would really make an impact.'

Involvement

Communities sharing households and resources have an important witness to society in their critical stance, healing ministry, and witness to an impossibility made possible.

Not everyone is called to live so closely together. But all of us are called to be salt in society. Living in community does not of itself achieve it; maintaining effective community life, as Clark pointed out, is often in great tension

11

with practising close involvement with society. But many Christians *are* linking together to engage more closely with issues in society.

In Washington, the members of the Sojourners Community bought a house in a down-town area to get to know impoverished black Americans. In England, the Evangelical Race Relations Group and missionary societies are meeting the challenge of the National Front by developing positive relationships with coloured communites. In Leeds the 'Whole Story Festival' (1977) spawned new fellowship between suburban Christians and black Christian churches in Chapeltown. A Christian group was formed to meet leaders of the Moslem and Sikh communities. The Festival of Light rallies, the marches of the Peace People for Northern Ireland in 1976–77, and the Anti-Racism marches of early 1978 were all found by many Christians to be occasions for taking to the streets to make an impact on public opinion. The Mayflower Centre in London, Shrewsbury House in Everton, Liverpool, and the OK Club in Kilburn, London, all developed community centres to give, to those living in the 'concrete jungle', a place to belong to.

These ventures predated the emergence of the term 'radical discipleship'. The substance of this discipleship was forged not in the theological colleges nor the suburban churches but on the anvil of experience, when obedient Christians faced head-on the stark questions of society. Housing problems, poverty, social deprivation, discrimination and unemployment challenged them to dig deep into the resources of biblical faith. The results are emerging in the publications of the Frontier Youth Trust, the Latin American Theological Fraternity, and the Shaftesbury Project. While we must beware of producing many words and no action, it is nonetheless because of the dearth of involvement until recently that Christians are discussing, and moving with care, as they enter new fields.

What is emerging is not a blueprint for action but a style of doing things. Christians are discovering that the true community of the church challenges assumptions of society such as the distribution of wealth, social anonymity, power structures, stratification between national, racial and social groups, and the marginalisation of those who are seen to be useless or irrelevant to the prevailing social structures.

The lifestyle of many individuals points a prophetic path. Roger Dowley is little known to English evangelicals. At the end of the war, as a Baptist layman setting up in legal practice, he opted to live in the East End of London rather than the blossoming suburbia. His children went to local schools, experiencing all the 'deprivation' of the inner city. Now two of them have PhD's. American research has shown that children brought up in monochrome suburbia are less fitted to deal with the ups and downs of life than those exposed to the rough-and-tumble of the inner city. The less gifted may not get PhD's – but while Christians are single, or have only young children, why can they not support Christian mission in deprived areas by living there?

Charity and justice

Christian involvement often follows the example of the good Samaritan, by bringing immediate relief to obvious crises. In a world where Indians ignore a person collapsing in a bus queue for fear of losing their own place, Americans ignore a girl attacked on the street because they do not wish to 'get involved', the English ignore all forms of Asian hospitality and politness to Asian immigrants, and Marxists and revolutionaries denounce all 'charity' as counter-revolutionary – the help an individual gives to an individual carries real weight.

Loving our neighbour is not something we can leave to the government to do for us. We cannot wait for the revolution to miraculously produce a world where no wrongs exist to be righted. Love shown in cases of need has its own witness, and it serves the felt need of real people. No political structures are altered and no lessening of the death rate is achieved by the work of Mother Teresa, caring for the dying in Calcutta; but is it therefore better to leave these skeletal wrecks of human flesh to die alone? Her orphanage does not solve the population problem – but James Gustafson, a professor of ethics from Chicago, com-

13

mented after a visit that the children were far more alert, responsive and loving than any others he had seen in Calcutta.

Christian relief workers in India after the cyclone in Andhra Pradesh in November 1977 could not prevent another cyclone. But militant Hindus and Marxists asked members of the Evangelical fellowship of India Commission on Relief well-cleaning project, 'Why are you doing this?'

Students at St. John's College, Nottingham, could not influence the course of the fireman's strike in 1977 one way or the other; but they operated a firewatching service on a nearby council estate.

Charity is a biblical mandate.

Too often, however, Christians have restricted their involvement to that level. But God demands justice in society, and many injustices have their roots deep in social structures. Michael Eastman of the Frontier Youth Trust writes:

> Picking up the casualties leads to investigating the causes. Why? Why? Why? What's wrong with an educational system that turns out a proportion of young people labelled 'failures' before they begin? Who decides to bulldoze a whole district and put streets on end? Why should the pits close or the docks move or the factory shut?[7]

A survey[8] by François Houtart of 6,700 projects benefitting 25,000,000 people run by the Roman Catholic Church in India and funded from abroad, revealed that relatively few of the projects questioned the prevailing social, economic and political arrangements that keep people poor. Relatively few projects aimed to secure for the people the rights guaranteed for them in the constitution. Yet poverty is intimately linked with social patterns: landholding, authoritarianism, and the people's ignorance of their rights and dignity.

Evangelical Christians round the world are increasingly recognising the importance of tackling the cases of injustice as part of Christian mission. Dr Sylvia Babu is involved in Christian community health programmes in India. She says: 'In the past, village outreach programmes for health

14

care have done nothing much except foster systems which keep people poor. We have given people religion to hold on to, but we have not worked with them for their basic rights. More of us are now trying to get involved with changing these systems and to make people aware of their rights.'

The Madras Declaration on Evangelical Social Action produced in 1979 by evangelicals throughout India states:

> Whereas God's mission to establish his kingdom included forgiveness for sins and reconciliation with God in the context of social justice, we have failed to see that the scope of God's mission delivers the poor from their destitution, challenges unjust structures and systems and demonstrates new economic, social and political relationships in the life of the community of the King. (For full text see appendix 3)

The movement for radical discipleship gained visibility and impetus at the Lausanne Congress in 1974. In the Lausanne Covenant, evangelicals committed themselves to work for justice and develop a simple lifestyle. World-wide study groups were set up to develop the meaning of this commitment. Their concluding conference in 1980 produced an Evangelical Commitment to Simple Lifestyle which stated:

> Poverty and excessive weath, militarism and the arms industry and the unjust distribution of capital, land and resources are issues of power and powerlessness. Without a shift of power through structural change these problems cannot be solved.

We should not separate and oppose charity and justice. Neither should we confuse them. The prophets demanded both individual charity and social justice, as we shall see.

The life and worship of the Christian community

Christians are discovering that shared community and resources, and mutual involvement in social issues, communicate Christ's love and deliverance to many needs today: a sense of belonging, a simple lifestyle, an attack on the causes of social injustice, a demonstration of an alternative way of life. This brings pressure on mutual relation-

15

ships within Christian groups as more is given and more demanded in commitment. It brings pressure on people's relationship with God, for such a new lifestyle is a fruit of his Spirit alone. Are the church's resources in worship, fellowship-patterns and decision-making adequate for the needs of those seeking to draw more deeply on each other and on God? Are regular attendance at a 'tramcar' fellowship, in a hymn-prayer sandwich-service dominated by one man, and occasional visits to the midweek Bible study sufficient to feed Christian relationships? Are matins and sermon and quarterly PCC meetings good enough structures of learning and decision-making, to develop Christian ministry and discover Christian responses to the questions of contemporary witness? When growth is taking place in these areas of learning and response, it is very often taking place outside traditional structures. But, Howard Snyder demands, when will we recognise that the urgent business of God is bypassing these structures? They need renewal if they are not to stifle further growth. New wine needs new wineskins.

Renewal is changing the structures of many churches, not only in response to the demands of their mission, but as a result of the ferment of the Holy Spirit within the Body of Christ. This has been largely associated with the Charismatic Movement. Renewal is transforming worship, correcting the balance between head and heart, mind and body, leadership and participation, intellect and emotion. Emotional warmth, contributions from many members, the use of touch in expressing life in Christ through handshake or embrace, use of the body in praise, dance and drama, the exercise of spiritual gifts, an emphasis on songs of praise flowing from a revival in Christian song-writing, and prayer in small groups during a worship service – all are restoring a balance which was heavily loaded in favour of one-way, pulpit-to-pew, parent-child communication of intellectual ideas.

The experience of renewal in the Spirit is also transforming our ideas of ministry. The rediscovery of the Spirit's gifts, exercised through the members of the Body for the

16

good of the whole, has redefined the task of ministry – 'entering the ministry' always was an erroneous description of the task of teaching a leading Christian congregation, but it continues to dominate the understanding of pastors, clergy and congregations. Ministry is what 'he' does up in the pulpit every Sunday, or what 'he' does in evangelising, counselling and helping. The whole question of whether 'she' can do it too is related to this misunderstanding of the role of 'he'.

The Spirit has himself led the revolt against his imprisonment and the imprisonment of his gifts in his people. More people are realising that natural and supernatural gifts are given to each member for the good of the whole in fellowship, mutual caring for each other and outsiders, and worship. Some ministries exist for the discerning, co-ordinating and educating of the ministries of others. It is not the ministry of a superstar pastor, omnicompetent or omnipresent. It is the ministry of a shared leadership-group.

St. Michael's Church, York, is an example of one man, with a great evangelistic gift, nevertheless developing a pattern of leadership focused on an elders' group. This shared the burdens and the decisions of leadership, and extended its scope. For example, one family in the church asked the elders' group for guidance on whether to pursue Christian service in Canada. The vicar himself would not take on outside engagements without consulting the group. In St. John's Church, Bangalore, we are also discovering the richness and potential of working as a team in ministry.

In his paper for the National Evangelical Anglican Congress in 1977, *Mission and Ministry*, Michael Green wrote:

> We never find a presbyter in the singular in the New Testament. He is always a member of a team . . . The plurality of leadership facilitates pastoral care, encourages stimulus and fresh thinking, and offsets the pecularities of any one leader.[9]

The Congress called the church to give recognition to the place of women in such shared leadership – though not necessarily to give them the chairman's role.

When the church's practice of ministry is biblical, it

makes a vital impact on society. The biblical pattern of ministry is that leadership is servanthood. Many hierarchical leadership patterns in the world are based on having as many people as possible as one's servants. The democratic pattern owes much to the biblical concept that the leader serves as many people as possible. The biblical pattern of ministry is that women are also given the Spirit's gifts without discrimination. The church's ministry is not complete unless women exercise their gifts. In society, women participate on terms laid down by men. When the church has encouraged the gifts of women, she has been able to change those situations in society which reduce women to an inferior position and to economic and sexual exploitation.

What is the difference?

How does a Christian group with concern for society and an understanding of itself as a community differ, in its goal, programme and organisation, from any group with an active social conscience? Are we in danger of turning the church into a social services agency?

If the church is to be involved in social service, it will provide some common answers to common questions. Tear Fund drills wells; so does Oxfam. One difference is that there are personal repercussions for each member of the church. Integrity demands a revised lifestyle in our homes, a refusal to delegate responsibility to paid professionals to do all the caring on our behalf. The existence of the church as a community, witnessing to the deliverance and power of God in its own experience, relationships and worship is central to its role in God's plan for society. (See chapter 5)

Many Christian groups are realising that at crucial points they must differ from secular society in the way they analyse and address the problems of people and communities. They fear that too often Christians have unthinkingly adopted the individualism of the West or the fatalism of the East, the attitudes, analyses and programmes of their own culture. As they tackle these problems, these groups are bringing the issues that face them to the Bible.

18

They face the world of suffering squarely and ask: 'If the Christian God made the world, and if he is revealed in Scripture, what resources does the biblical tradition have for responding to him in this situation? What does God enable and require us to do?' They want to know what the good news is that Jesus has for the poor, the powerless and the exploited. They want to communicate that news to people in their personal economic, social and political relationships.

An important evangelical report on communicating the gospel in different situations states:

> Today's readers (of the Bible) cannot come to the text in a personal vacuum, and should not try to. Instead they should come with an awareness of concerns stemming from their cultural background, personal situation and responsibility to others. These concerns will influence the questions that are put to the Scriptures. What is received back, however, will not be answers only, but more questions. As we address Scripture, Scripture addresses us.[10]

The challenges of radical discipleship

The centre of gravity of world Christianity has shifted to the Two Thirds World, according to Professor Andrew Walls of Aberdeen University. Here live the largest number of Christians, the fastest growing churches, the majority of the poor and most of those who do not know Christ. Many Christians in the Two Thirds World are facing up to real situations of distress, injustice and conflict. Christians in the west are also realising that they are part of a world-wide family most of whom are coloured and poor. They are also becoming more alive to the existence of powerlessness and deprivation in their own countries. Those living in situations of privilege are beginning to realise they are also part of the problem. As Thomas Cullinan puts it:

> It we idolise wealth, then we create poverty; if we idolise success, them we create the inadequate; if we idolise power, then we create powerlessness.[11]

These groups are finding that they cannot meet the needs

of the world by addressing an impersonal message to people's minds. Neville Black of the Evangelical Urban Training Project said at the NEAC Congress in 1977: 'If we are not meeting the needs of the poor, our Gospel is phoney'. Roger Sainsbury, the warden of the Mayflower Centre, said:

> Our Jesus has been too small, our understanding of the cross too limited. The formula of individual salvation from personal guilt and frustration has meant that the Gospel has become irrelevant to the working class . . . We need to think again about the Gospel we are communicating.[12]

Such groups are finding that they must take stances for justice for the poor, for sharing, for breaking down social barriers and for calling people to be disciples of Jesus in socially relevant ways as servants. They are discovering what it means to walk the way of Jesus, the word in working clothes. For example, the Manifesto of the Evangelical Coalition for Urban Mission (Birmingham 1981) declares:

> We must actively express God's demands for love, justice and reconciliation throughout society and for liberation of all people from every form of oppression, poverty and discrimination . . . So we commit ourselves . . . to identify and challenge in Christ's name, the oppressive and demonic in individuals, communities and institutions, to join hands with all who own Jesus as Lord in making real among urban people the new community of righteousness, peace and joy to which the Holy Spirit is calling us all.

These groups identify their stance as one of radical discipleship. This style appeals because it demands the personal integrity of a simple lifestyle. It gives personal significance in a committed community in a world where individuals are free to do their own thing at the cost of isolation and insignificance. It brings a costly challenge in a world of easy conformity to 'the system'.

It emphasises group significance, in a world where people know their own powerlessness. It involves submission in every part of life to the lordship of Christ, and service under Christ's lordship in the whole of human life, and in a world of compartmentalised living and thinking.

God has been at work in Christians' lives, using their experiences as his mouthpiece. The questions and style of radical discipleship are growing out of experience in social involvement and experience of the Holy Spirit's renewal. New questions are being asked of the Bible: What truths about God and man are being uncovered?

And a theme, peripheral to much Christian thinking, but central to the work and life of Jesus Christ is emerging: the kingdom of God.

3: The ministry of Jesus
A whole Gospel for a whole world

Thank God for the Bible. It prevents us from believing that a particular expression of Christianity is the only possible expression of the teaching of Jesus. The truth in Jesus is free to judge and correct us. It is free to debate with new questions posed by our historical circumstances. The truth is to set us free from the blinkers and bonds of our times. So we should not imprison the truth in one historical expression of obedience, for we will only imprison ourselves in irrelevant legalism. The truth will always break out.

Radical discipleship tries to discover the resources in Jesus' ministry for questions of Christian obedience today.

> What is the gospel for urban, industrialised secular men and women? What is God's purpose in sending his servants into the world as it is? What kind of Christian community is flexible, open, adaptable and courageous enough to embody the gospel and express this purpose? What is meant by the Kingdom of God and how is his reign expressed? What is God's intention for man in society both now and in the future?[1]

The Kingdom of God

Jesus' prime concern was the kingdom of God. Mark launches Jesus on to the stage of world history with these words: 'After John had been put in prison, Jesus went to Galilee and preached the Good News from God. "The right time has come," he said, "and the Kingdom of God is near! Turn away from your sins and believe the Good News." Jesus counselled his disciples to 'seek first God's kingdom and his righteousness', and to pray 'thy kingdom come', which he explains as 'thy will be done on earth as it is in heaven.'

The kingdom is God's programme of total redemption for every aspect of creation. The good news, according to Matthew and Mark, begins with an unbroken chain of healings. Jesus cures lepers, blind men, people demon-possessed, a woman with a haemorrhage, and a centurion's servant. The kingdom invades the old age of our everyday world where sickness and evil destroy God's good creation. Jesus' miracles were the presence of God's kingdom bringing wholeness to men's bodies, and a foretaste of bodily resurrection. The kingdom is a treasure chest of themes of God's deliverance – creation, new life, forgiveness, healing, new birth, redemption, a new lifestyle and resurrection.

The kingdom is a common element in Jesus' situation and ours. How do we link a message spelt out in terms relevant to a limited agrarian society with the problems of living in a technological global village? In Jesus' ministry God's kingdom invaded. It found expression in liberated relationships which acutely challenged the distorted personal, social, economic and religious relationships which express rebellion against God. God's kingdom is his ongoing invasion of liberation. Our task is to express its new relationships in terms relevant to today's societies.

What does God's kingdom of right relationships look like? If the kingdom is where God's will is done on earth, what will happen then? The kingdom was the Old Testament hope for a transformed world, so it is there we must begin.

The Old Testament Promise

God chose the people of Israel to be a light to the nations: to show the rest of the world what God was like, through their lifestyle. God took the role of film director; the history of Israel was to be his masterpiece. The director is never seen, but the whole film reflects his character and attitudes.

God is just; he hates oppression. Israel traced its origin to God's deliverance of Jacob's descendants from slave labour, a forced birth control policy and ruthless repression.

23

When Israel herself became wealthy and unjust, God judged her in turn. God's goal was to liberate his people from evil, to be free to serve him. Spiritual liberation and material liberation go together.

But Israel misrepresented God. She tolerated oppression, injustice and paganism in her national life. To vindicate his name, God had to judge her. So Exodus ended in exile and the need of a deeper liberation became clear. Material liberation without spiritual liberation is a dead end.

God continually intervened to save his people from the consequence of their rebellion through military means. He used Cyrus, a military conqueror, to end their exile. But God's final solution, announced in Isaiah 40–55, was to deliver his people from this deeper rebellion by a servant who would not fight, but suffer; not inflict violence, but absorb it.

When God's people experienced this spiritual liberation, they would be the light to draw other nations to God. So total would this liberation be that it would transform the whole created order. God would create a new heaven (a new spiritual sphere) and a new earth. The prophets had visions of this new world. Jeremiah glimpsed a new relationship between God and man: man would enjoy doing God's will (Jer. 31:31–34). Joel foresaw God pouring out his Spirit on all flesh (Joel 2:28–29). Ezekiel looked forward to the forgiveness of sins and a new shepherd king for Israel (Ezek. 36:24–29). Isaiah promised that the deaf, blind, lame and dumb would be healed and streams break out in the desert (Isa. 35:3–6). Daniel divined that all God's people would enjoy this new world, and held out hope of the resurrection of the dead (Dan. 12:2–3). When all this took place on the 'Day of the Lord' God's reign would be established, his kingdom complete. There would be total *shalom*: peace, harmony, righteousness, justice, well-being. Right relationships all round, in a new material order free of sickness and death. God's liberation would be total, spiritual and material.

The Jews hoped that glory-day would come for them when they got back to Jerusalem after the exile. It didn't, and so over the centuries they concluded all they could do was wait till it happened. Some (the Pharisees) argued that it would only come when Israel was perfectly obedient to all God's laws for one day. So they made the requirements of the strict laws of purity for the priests to apply to all Israelite people, and restricted membership of the people of God to those who really kept the law. The common people, the lost sheep, were disinherited. The Zealots wanted to give God a helping hand by routing the defiling Gentiles from their land by violence: because the Jews tolerated the Roman-Gentiles God's kingdom had not come. The Essenes just moved out, and camped by the Dead Sea – separating themselves from sources of contamination as they, the elect people, waited for the kingdom. The Sadducees were the ruling group, consisting of the high priests, the nobles, the most eminent citizens and the leading men. They were supported by the wealthy, but had no following among the common people. They held on to their power by collaborating with the Roman government. The religious, the nationalists, the pure and the powerful sat and waited. Some day, some way, history would end and they would be safe.

Jesus' shock news was that God's kingdom had arrived ahead of time. Its powers and blessings were unleashed on the world through his work. Men were invited to enter it now, especially the poor, forgotten, and disinherited lost sheep of Israel: the lawbreakers, the impure and the powerless. By teaching and healing, proclaiming forgiveness, calling men to repent and enter the kingdom, driving out demons, healing the sick, and raising the dead, Jesus demonstrated that the spiritual and physical liberation of the kingdom was present. God was giving men a foretaste of the kingdom that would one day remake the whole world.

Physical and spiritual liberation went together. Jesus announced his work as 'good news to the poor, liberation to the captives, sight to the blind, freedom to the oppressed

25

an announcement that the time has come for God to save his people' (Luke 4:18–19). This echoes Isaiah's version of liberation from captivity in Babylon and the Jubilee liberation of land and people from debt. Jesus' liberation will be the final liberation of history, and the total one. John sent disciples from his prison cell to find out from Jesus if he was the one whom John foretold, who would bring God's forgiveness and Spirit. Jesus' reply was to continue healing the blind, diseased, plagued and demon-possessed (Luke 7:18–23). Physical healing was a sign and a part of liberation in the kingdom.

God's reign was invading, to bring physical and spiritual deliverance. 'It is by means of God's power that I drive out demons; and this proves that the kingdom of God has already come to you. When a strong man, with all his weapons ready, guards his own house, all his belongings are safe. But when a stronger man attacks him and defeats him, he carries away all the weapons the owner was depending on and divides up what he stole' (Luke 11:20–21). The kingdom did not just invade in a spiritual, non-material way: that would be to separate physical and spiritual in a way foreign to the Bible. But the full completion of God's deliverance, both spiritual and physical, remains till the future. The disciples were to pray 'thy kingdom come'.

Right Relationships

The kingdom of God and his righteousness includes all the right relationships that will characterise the final kingdom. The kingdom now transforms all human relationships, the relationships between people and God, people and people, and people and the physical world. This is God's *shalom*.

Jesus mediated a new relationship between God and man. He taught his disciples a new word for God, never found in any Jewish prayer: 'Abba' – 'Daddy', Father. At the last supper he announced that his blood would seal the new covenant of the forgiveness of sins. He made forgiveness of others an acid test for his company of forgiven people. John the Baptist announced, Jesus promised and the Day of Pentecost heralded the gift of the Holy Spirit, the very presence of God in men's lives. In Jewish thought, sonship, forgiveness and the Spirit belonged to the kingdom of God at the end of history; not to this world.

Jesus brought new relationships between people. The prophetic hope of the kingdom was of a new king at the head of a redeemed community. Jesus summoned the people of Israel to submit to God's rule and be renewed in their national life by repenting and entering the kingdom. The focus of this renewal was a group obedient to Jesus: they were to be the salt of the earth and the light of the world, to fulfil the role assigned to Israel. This group was to live out the transformed relationships of the kingdom.

Various factions within Judaism excluded 'the people of the land' from membership of God's people, because they associated with Gentiles or were in some way defiled. They had no time to keep all the detailed ritual laws for eating because they had to earn a living: they mixed with Gentiles because they took part in business or trade. A number of trades were thought to be necessarily immoral, so shopkeepers and physicians were thought necessarily dishonest, tailors were thought immoral because they had contact with women, even those whose trade involved foul smells such as tanners found themselves included among the common people 'who do not know the law and are accursed' (John 7:49). Fervent nationalists especially hated the tax-collectors who extorted the tribute which paid for heathen temples. All sick and diseased people were thought to be suffering for their sins. Lepers, the untouchables were cursed by God and a potent source of physical and ritual defilement. Women were second-class citizens and kept separate from male company because men trusted no-one with their sisters, daughters or wives. And the less said about prostitutes, and those half-breed Jews the Samaritans, the better . . .

Enter Jesus! He mingled with the people of the land, told them parables and sat at table with them. He said they were welcome members of the new people of God. He undermined the whole Pharisaic concept of God's people by describing unclean people as members of God's holy family.

He fraternised with traitors by eating with public enemies number one, the tax-collectors. He brought radical change to the lives of Matthew and Zaccheus and welcomed them to a new company which included their former victims, hardworking fishermen like Peter and John.

He did not leave the sick to suffer and endure their God-given fate. He healed them. He touched the lepers, unafraid of their defilement, and restored them to human society.

Jesus' company was remarkable for its female membership. In the kingdom mens' hardness of heart is cured, purity rules their gaze and the power of lust is controlled. So Mary the prostitute and Peter the faithful husband find themselves together in Jesus' company. Luke records the band of women who were last at the cross and first at the tomb.

Jesus further antagonised Jewish feeling by including the Samaritans. He talked with a Samaritan woman and drew attention to the gratitude of a Samaritan leper he had healed. He ridiculed Jewish religious callousness to suffering by holding up as an example of God's concern, a good Samaritan. It was as foolish as speaking to a National Front meeting about the patriotism of a black Englishman – and as politically relevant.

For this was God's *shalom* taking concrete form against the rebellion of man in his social relationships. Jesus ensured his redeemed community of transformed relationships challenged and crossed all the social divisions of the day. Nicodemus the pious Jew and Matthew the traitor, hardworking men like James and John, and Mary the prostitute – all had to accept and love each other if they belonged to Jesus. Unclean and unnamed people of the land, Samaritans, officers of the Roman occupying forces and Gentiles, all were welcome. Jesus brought people from these deeply divided groups to demonstrate that the reality of the kingdom was shown in the way new human relationships were forged and nourished between people separated by the sinful barriers of sex, race, class, caste, wealth, power and tradition.

Their community was to demonstrate freedom from greed, hate, resentment, lust and the will to dominate others. He taught them not to retaliate; to forgive, to help anyone in need whose path they crossed, to share their goods and to be at all times servants. John Yoder beautifully describes their character.

> When he called his society together, Jesus gave its members a new way of life to live. He gave them a new way to deal with money – by sharing it. He gave them a new way to deal with the problems of leadership – by drawing on the gift of every member, even the most humble. He gave them a new way to deal with a corrupt society – by building a new order, not smashing the old. He gave them a new pattern of relationships between man and woman, between parent and child, between master and slave, in which was made concrete a radical new vision of what it means to be a human person.[2]

Political Implications

While Jesus' message was not a political theory of democracy, his programme had profound political implications. Ron McMullen defines a political act as 'one where there is an effort to preserve or change what exists in social systems.'[3] Jesus did not seem anxious to preserve many traditions of the Jewish social systems. His new society was an outright challenge to religious and social oppression in Jewish society.

The Jewish leaders believed the kingdom of God, their national deliverance, would come when the whole people of God kept the whole law of God for one day. All those who did not minutely follow religious and social laws and observances were despised, rejected and marginalised. The 'sinners' who followed immoral trades included adulterers, swindlers, excise-men, shepherds, donkey drivers, pedlars and tanners as well as tax-collectors. The people of the land 'who do not know the law and are accused' made up sixty to eighty per cent of the population. In the leaders' eyes, none of them belonged to God's people.

Jesus specifically welcomed into the people of God the uneducated, the economically poor, the lepers and the sick, the children and the women, and the other social outcasts of Jewish society. His meals with sinners meant they were invited to share in the banquet of the kingdom foreseen by Isaiah.

Jewish leaders based their superiority on their adherence to the law. The law was the basis of Israel's desire to be free of Gentile defilement, and of their hope of final victory. Those who flouted the law were national traitors: had not the Jewish martyrs consented to be slain on the Sabbath rather than break the law and fight? Observance of the Sabbath was a badge of Jewish identity. Jesus challenged these interpretations of the law that degraded people and denied them God's help and human dignity. He broke the Sabbath law because it prevented men doing good to the sick and needy. He said that the Sabbath was made for man. The Jews had dehumanised the Sabbath law. Jesus told the Pharisees that they totally misinterpreted and dehumanised the law by tithing garden herbs while allowing unjust merciless practices to flourish.

Jesus gave the impression of usurping Moses' supreme position as Israel's lawgiver, by contradicting current traditions of interpretation. According to Jesus, those traditions isolated the law from the socio-economic context in which it had been given to promote just human relationships, and especially justice for the poor. The interpreters of the law tried to obey the law in such a way that they could avoid clashes with Roman social, political and economic concerns. Vinay Samuel writes 'Once the interpreters of the law make the practice of the law designed to protect the poor, bearable for themselves, the poor lose the protection of the law.'[4] When the rich young ruler met Jesus, he declared that he had kept all the commandments of the law. But he had obeyed an *interpretation* of it without its central concern for justice for the poor. It was this that Jesus pointed out to him. Above all Jesus gave the true meaning of the law. It means love for neighbour, for enemy, for the poor. He demonstrated *his* interpretation by living it – by healing the poor, eating with the social outcasts and national enemies, and welcoming women to his company. By his teaching, by his practice, and by forming a new people of God Jesus deeply challenged the religious and social structures of Israel, because they were unjust. He told the people of the land that all God's blessings denied by their leaders were available to them. He claimed to teach the law, but he ate with lawbreakers and castigated the recognised guardians of the law for hypocrisy, violence and selfishness. He formed a new social entity of God's people – the group of disciples, and chose twelve new symbolic heads for the twelve tribes of Israel. He prophesied the destruction of the Temple, which was not only the centre of Jewish religious and national sentiment. It embraced the functions of the Treasury, the Bank of England and the Stock Exchange, and it was the seat of government where the Sanhedrin met. The Temple had considerable power in the economy, provided wealth for the priests and was a source of economic exploitation. Jesus made a highly significant display of God's displeasure by clearing out the moneychangers.

In Jewish society religion and politics were inseparable. By attacking the religious leaders and the law, by declaring God's help and favour to the poor, by mingling with social outcasts and calling them into God's kingdom, Jesus challenged the religious and social structures that denied dignity and rights to many members of God's people.

His own new society held up a mirror of judgement by creating new relationships of righteousness between men and women, Jew and non-Jew, master and slave, rich and poor.

Roman Power

So far we have seen how Jesus combated the social and political systems of the Jewish state in Palestine. But what was his stance in relation to Rome?

Rome was the source of political power for the Jewish puppets and collaborators. Roman power was based on domination, on the view that the strong should use their power to enrich themselves and subdue others. Jesus re-

31

jected this concept. In contrast to Roman commanders who entered cities in triumph with horses and chariots, he made his triumphal entry on a donkey. He presented himself to Pilate as a king without soldiers. He did not co-operate with those who maintained power through domination and who were responsible for existing social patterns. He often refused to justify his actions to authorities who questioned him, during both his ministry and his trial.

Jesus judged the social patterns of Roman power by God's standards. Far from dividing the world into two separate realms – Caesar's and God's – he regarded everything that happened in the whole creation, the rainfall, the growth of flowers and the feeding patterns of birds and men, as subject to the rule and power of God. Richard Cassidy concludes:

> The only areas in which Caesar can expect allegiance are those in which his patterns are in conformity with God's desired patterns . . . there is no area in which God's desires can be rightfully neglected. Indeed God must be rendered to, even if to do so requires a rejection of the practices that the Caesars have themselves set in place.[5]

We see specific working out of Jesus' view in his teaching on leadership. He renounced leadership through domination and instead advocated servanthood (Mark 10:42–45). In the parable of the talents (Matt. 25:14–30), Jesus commended the servants who used all the resources they were gifted with for the master's use (and so for the benefit of others). The servants were not all given equal resources, nor were they rewarded with personal possession and control of their gains. Instead all used whatever resources they had for another, and were rewarded with greater responsibilities. Such a leadership pattern gives a place for every member of the community to use their gifts for the service of all. It was institutionalised in the patterns of gifts and ministry developed in the early church. Such a leadership pattern gives power to everyone who renounces domination to serve others. Such a leadership pattern was integral to Jesus' idea that his community would find its members in the highways and byways, among the outcasts and the poor, and that among the most important members of the community would be the weakest–children.

Jesus here pointed a way to a social order where no oppressing groups could hold sway, for all members would be servants. He trained his disciples in a social system which had it been widely accepted would have brought about the end of the Roman Empire. And history records that eventually, it did.

Health and Economics

The kingdom brings new relationships in the material sphere. The Old Testament hope looked for a transformed world, a new abundant earth, people liberated from physical disease and ultimately resurrection. In his healing ministry and in raising people from the dead Jesus brought this aspect of the kingdom and commissioned his disciples to 'preach the kingdom of God and to heal' (Luke 9:2; Mark 6:12–13). The invasion of the kingdom transforms the physical creation itself.

The kingdom also affects economic relationships. We see Jesus' concern, that the justice and righteousness of the kingdom take shape in human society, especially in his concern for the poor.

'Blessed are the poor.' Jesus' words are the first recorded praise of the poor in history. The gospels do not idealise them; the poor are associated with the blind, the lame, the deaf, lepers, prisoners, the oppressed and the dead. They are not just economically poor, but on account of their economic condition they cannot obtain justice. They are victims of the powerful and the violent. They cannot stand up for themselves, and no one will stand up for them except God. So the poor are particularly aware of their dependence on him.

An international evangelical study on the term 'poor' in the New Testatment concludes that the term refers to:

The manual worker who struggles to survive on a day-to-day basis, the destitute cowering as a beggar, the one reduced to meekness, the one brought low . . . those weak and tired from carrying heavy burdens, the leper and very often 'the common people' . . . the majority of references indicate that the poor are the mercilessly oppressed, the powerless, the destitute, the downtrodden . . . it had been the rich who accommodated to the religious and social demands of the Greek and Roman overlords. The poor tended to remain faithful to God. Some rich actually became poor because of their faithfulness. So the poor and the faithful became the same. There is no indication that in this use (of 'poor in spirit' in Matthew 5:3) economic realities were excluded.[6]

The distorted relationship between poor and rich is an example of man's sin and rebellion: largely the rebellion of the rich. Wealth in the gospels is a grave spiritual danger. It blinds a man's eyes to the values of the kingdom, it twists his priorities and is the major distraction to the true service of God. It chokes the seed of the word, and blinds him to the needs of the poor.

Jesus gave no new revelation on poverty and wealth. In the parable of Dives and Lazarus, he emphasised that Moses and the prophets contained sufficient teaching on the topic. God is just. 'The Lord does not show partiality, and he does not accept bribes. He makes sure that the orphans and widows are treated fairly; he loves the foreigners who live with our people, and gives them food and clothes. So then, show love for these foreigners, because you were once foreigners in Egypt' (Deut. 10:17–19). God requires justice and so takes particular interest in those most likely to be taken advantage of. He requires his people to show the same concern because God delivered them from oppression in Egypt.

When people get rich it may be because of injustice. 'Evil men live among my people: they lie in wait like men who spread nets to catch birds, but they have set their traps to catch men. Just as a hunter fills his cage with birds, they have filled their houses with loot. That is why they are powerful and rich, why they are fat and well fed. There is no limit to their evil deeds. They do not give orphans their rights or show justice to the oppressed' (Jer. 5:26–28). Because such injustice went unchecked among God's people, especially by the king, God sent them into exile. 'The Lord told me to give this message to the royal house of Judah, the descendants of David: "Listen to what I, the Lord, am saying. See that justice is done everyday. Protect the person who is being cheated from the one who is cheating him. If you don't, the evil you are doing will make my anger burn like a fire that cannot be put out . . . I will punish you for what you have done. I will set your palace on fire, and the fire will burn down everything round it" ' (Jer. 21:11–14).

The hope for the kingdom of God was centred on a king who would see justice was done. 'He will judge the poor fairly, and defend the rights of the helpless' (Isa. 11:4). 'The Sovereign Lord has filled me with his spirit. He has chosen me and sent me to bring good news to the poor, to heal the broken-hearted, to announce release to the captives and freedom to those in prison' (Isa. 61:1).

Huge disparities between rich and poor existed in Jesus' time. Four families monopolised the revenues of the temple and filled the high priestly office. Jesus' parables parade before us large landowners, tenants who get into debt, widows who are taken advantage of, rich men who build bigger barns and feast sumptuously everyday. Jesus was outstanding not only for his fierce condemnation of the callous indifference of the rich but also for the way he apportioned his time, spending the majority of it in poor 'Galilee of the Gentiles'. He understood the value of a silver coin to a housewife, a mite to a widow, a jar of ointment to a prostitute, and a pig's husk to an unemployed youth.

Jesus' preoccupation with the poor validated his messianic ministry. The poor were the only group he singled out especially to receive the good news. Why? Because of their poverty and vulnerability, they had no other security and hope than God. They were particularly receptive to news that God's kingdom was open to them. The religious leaders made them outcasts unfit to belong to God's people: so Jesus extended God's invitation to the banquet of the kingdom to the poor, the crippled, the blind and the lame.

The news that God loved and wanted them gave them a dignity and self-worth their society denied them.

But the kingdom also brought material help to the poor. In entering the kingdom poor people joined a brotherhood whose economic relationships were to be a sign of the justice of the final kingdom, and a fulfilment of the Old Testament requirement that there should be no poor among the people of God. The Book of Acts records that there was no needy person among the Christian community, deliberately echoing an Old Testament phrase (Deut. 15:4).

How was this achieved? In the Old Testament specific mechanisms were instituted to prevent people being pauperised, a regular cancellation of debts, legislation against excessive interest on charitable loans, and provisions for the poor to share in the harvest. Thirty per cent of the tithe was set apart for the poor. In the New Testament the resources of the entire community were available to anyone in need. Jesus promised that food and clothes would be provided by God for all who sought his kingdom: that those who forsook worldly goods would receive a hundred-fold in this life: the disciples shared a common purse, and Luke records the contributions of some of the women. The Acts community made special provision for widows, and members sold land and houses as need arose to care for the needy.

The Acts experiment of sharing was not (as some hold) a failure. When the Jerusalem Christians stood in need of outside assistance, it was because a famine had hit Jerusalem. Far from abandoning the principle of sharing at this point, Paul extended it, beyond the Jerusalem community. He instituted sharing between the churches, so that all could have an opportunity to live as Jesus did, to become poor to make others rich (2 Cor. 8:1-9).

Care for the poor was not limited to the poor members of the Christian community. Jesus stressed the duty of almsgiving; that is, giving to the poor: rich converts were expected to share their goods with the poor. Jesus' words 'the poor you will always have with you' are not a fatalistic resignation to poverty. He spoke them in a context. When

Judas complains about the expense of the ointment poured over Jesus' feet, Jesus explains it as an appropriate act of devotion to him at the time of his preparation for burial. Similar acts of devotion when Jesus is no longer with them can be made to Jesus after his death in giving to the poor. For 'you will always have poor people with you, but you will not always have me' (Matt. 26:6–13). This identification between Jesus and the poor is also made at the climax of Jesus' teaching in the previous chapter of Matthew. In Matthew 25, he stressed that any service to the poor, hungry, naked or to those in prison was service to the Lord of the universe and an acid test of the reality of faith (for further discussion see chapter 8).

Conclusion

Jesus' ministry announced the invasion of God's kingdom into every aspect of human life. It brought *a new pattern of relationships* that expressed God's concern for righteousness and justice.

The new community of the kingdom expressed these new relationships, in terms relevant to social oppression sanctioned by religion and economic injustice. The method of expressing and securing just relationships will vary from period to period and culture to culture. For example, Ruth's gleaning may not be practical in modern industry, but legislation against excessive interest and the means to enforce it would profoundly affect the indebtedness of millions of Indian peasants to landlords and moneylenders.

Jesus' ministry also brought *the possibility of such relationships*. For injustice is but an expression of man's rebellion against God and his bondage to evil. Jesus bound the strong man of evil. His ministry was God's unique defeat of evil which gives both the possibility of, and pattern for, Christian conflict with all forms of evil. The pattern of God's redemption is the pattern for the redeemed life. Why that is so we now examine.

4: Jesus is Lord

Jesus is Lord! This was the battle cry of the church of the risen Jesus. The title is all-embracing. Jesus is Lord of all creation: he is victor over evil and death. He is one with God as creator and redeemer. He is Lord of every part of his servants' lives. He is Lord in the present and coming kingdom of God.

His path to the throne lay through rejection and suffering. Redemption through suffering proclaims his Lordship over all evil, suffering and death. His death and resurrection are both the gateway of the kingdom of God and the pattern of its life. Without the resurrection, his identification with man in his rebellion, his favour to the poor, and his resistance to personal, social and demonic evil ends in tragedy. Evil has the last word. Resistance is futile. Jesus' ministry, death and resurrection and the coming of the Spirit opened the kingdom to man.

Resurrection of the dead occupied the centre stage in the Jewish hope of the kingdom. The claim that one solitary man had risen before the end of the world, a man who tried to usurp God's role in bringing the kingdom and had died under his curse, was either scandalous – or the seal of God's approval that the kingdom had come through Jesus in history.

History is our address. The resurrection assures us that God is overcoming evil in history and will overcome it at the end. It assures us God vindicates the way of Jesus (and no other) in combating evil. The pattern of God's redemption from evil is the pattern for the redeemed life in triumphant conflict with evil. Radical discipleship follows the redemption path of resurrection through crucifixion. We are to take up the cross involved in identifying with the

38

victims of evil and in resisting evil where we find it. We can only win.

The resurrection is God's victory over death. In the Old Testament death is anything that spoils life or makes it unbearable: sickness, poverty or separation from God. The resurrection is God's triumph over all powers of death in life: physical death, the fear of death, the cycle of law, sin and death, injustice, disease and demon-possession. It is the first-fruits of the new creation, the new earth where death will be no more, when God's justice and righteousness will dwell, to be tasted now. God's power is loose in the world, bringing life out of all forms of death.

Jesus is Lord

The resurrection proclaims Jesus as Lord of all life and Lord over death. The earliest creed 'Jesus is Lord' identifies Jesus with God as redeemer-creator. Jesus is shown to be God's agent of redemption to bring his purpose in creation to fulfilment. So he is shown to be also the agent through whom God made the world. In the Old Testament the Israelites' experience of God as redeemer led them to claim his authority as creator over all nations. In the New Testament, faith in Jesus as creator arises out of experience of him as redeemer. He is the goal of everything: therefore he is also the source of everything. 'God created the whole universe through him and for him. Christ existed before all things, and in union with him all things have their proper place . . . He is the first born Son, who was raised from death, in order that he alone might have the first place in all things . . . God made peace (Shalom) through his Son's death on the cross and so brought back to himself all things, both on earth and in Heaven' (Col. 1:16–20).

So Jesus is Lord of redeemed creation. Redemption in Jesus does not separate us from creation: it reveals the goal and true meaning of it, it frees us to bring God's purpose for every aspect of creation to its true fulfilment. Redemption embraces it totally. It is God's *shalom* for all he has made. The church is where Jesus' Lordship is explicitly acknowledged and is to be fully expressed. Paul's hymn in

Colossians identifies Jesus the redeemer-creator as 'The head of his body, the church: he is the source of the body's life.' The Church's mission is to declare that Lordship over the whole created order, demonstrate what creation looks like when acknowledging its master, summon all people to acknowledge his Lordship and seek ways of ordering the world that best express the present Lordship of Jesus, the king of justice and righteousness, the prince of *Shalom*.

Discipleship of the Lord of redeemed creation involves sharing the good news; calling men to repent, believe and serve Jesus as Lord. It also means expressing his Lordship by concern for justice; what people eat, where they live and whether they have work. Radical discipleship calls men to acknowledge Jesus as Lord of their work and society, as well as their homes. It seeks to discover what it means to confess his Lordship in the concrete realities of the present. 'Through all creation Jesus Christ is Lord.'

Social Sin

But there are rebels. 'Demonic forces deny the Lordship of Christ and keep men less than fully human.' The radical discipleship statement at Lausanne put a theological finger on one of the most perplexing aspects of society today. Problems and suffering come to people not only through the perversity of individuals. The pressures of political and economic systems conspire to deny dignity, work, health and food to millions.

Racialism in Britain is one example. The recession in world trade (due itself to a number of factors), increasing competition from imported goods and a pattern of low investment in manufacturing industries have contributed to putting over two million people into dole queues by the end of 1980. Standards of living fall, fewer public funds are available for improving amenities. People begin to think that a scapegoat is needed. Who better than the one million black and brown Englishmen imported in the boom years to do the dirty jobs no one else wanted? Why not send them back and give their jobs to 'our own' people? Greg Forster highlights the problem in housing:

An area begins to 'go downhill'. At the same time West Indian or Indian residents begin to move in, and get blamed for the perceived decline in standards. The age of the property, and perhaps planning blight in the shadow of proposed redevelopment in the distant future, are forgotten: the town's image demands that slums go, and while they are going 'immigrants' get the blame. Those who are immediately on hand are seen as the cause of a problem, when they are its victims. Like the barium meal given before an X-ray, they show up a problem which is there, and everyone wishes it was not. No doctor would suggest that the barium caused the ulcer it reveals![1]

If not the immigrants, then who are to blame for racialism? The members of the National Front? They feel their jobs are threatened, their children's education impaired, and their houses devalued by immigrant neighbours. They get a poor deal in the cutting of society's cake, fear it will get worse and feel powerless to do anything. The politicians? They make fine statements about the multi-racial society, but how many of them live in a multi-racial area? The dwellers in suburbia? They see racialism and its attendant violence as a symptom of declining moral standards and probably condemn it. But in our shrinking economy the middle class have the best share of housing, facilities, jobs and education. They move out of the cities for the very reason that immigrants move in, 'to find a better 'ole.' So they contribute to the decline of inner-city housing values and facilities and deprive the worse-off areas of their power, stability and expertise.

To blame one group is easy and false. To blame individuals alone is unfair. We are involved in social sin here. It is perhaps easier and more comfortable to view it from a distance. The Green Revolution in India introduced new methods of farming to provide more and better food. Now the country has a surplus of 20 million tons of rice. But those who could afford to invest in Green Revolution technology were the landowners. They produced the food that would give the best returns – rice, the food of the rich. Production of the staple food for the landless labourers remained static. The Green Revolution applied a technological solution to hunger and ignored the realities of Indian social, economic and political power. The issue is not the production of more resources: it is the question of who owns what resources there are. Professor C. T. Kurien of Madras writes in *Poverty and Development*, 'A pre-condition for the abolition of poverty in our country is the redistribution of resources and decision-making power in the system.'[2]

What price now the domino-theory of social change? Can we really continue to believe that if we can convert enough individuals to be honest hard-working Christians, we will produce a reformed and just society? South Africa has a very high percentage of born-again Christians, yet her society is not renowned for justice. Must we not look to the structures of society as well? But these are so complex – what can an individual or a minority group do?

We are again forced back to the Bible with new questions. How can we understand these social forces? How do they relate to the Lordship of Jesus? Is there a theology of social evil? This is 'inductive' study. It follows the theological method of Scripture where the people of God found themselves challenged to obedience in new situations and had to seek God's word afresh; for example, the entry of Gentile converts into the Church posed hard questions to the understanding of the law (Acts 15, and Paul's letters). Bruce Kaye writes in the introduction to the NEAC study book *The Changing World*:

> Traditionally, evangelicals have done their theology by trying to work out the basic principles from the Scriptures and then by either applying these scriptural principles to the question under discussion or seeking to discover their practical implications . . . Here an issue in the present situation has been taken, and then analysed in depth to see what is at stake in it and how Christian truth may be related to it.[3]

The Family of Man

The scriptural evidence is that moral and spiritual realities underlie the decisions that leaders, groups and people make each day.

The first is that man is a collective being as well as an individual one. He cannot escape the privileges, responsibilities and liabilities of belonging to society. The children of those who escaped from Egypt wandered in the desert because of their parents' murmuring against God. The nation lost a battle because of Achan's theft, and all Achan's family suffered for his wrong. The wise men of Proverbs taught the trainee leaders that 'righteousness makes a nation great; sin is a disgrace to any nation' (Prov. 14:34). In the book of Revelation, John points out the shortcomings of the seven churches and the sinfulness of nations. There is corporate responsibility and shared guilt for collective sin.

God judges people both for their conscious individual acts and for their participation in evil social structures. Amos condemns sexual misconduct and legalised oppression (Amos 2:6–7), corrupt legal systems that allow the wealthy to buy release but impose long sentences on the poor (Amos 5:10–15) and rich ladies whose social life and fine clothes depend on the sweat and tears of toiling peasants (Amos 4:1–2). The God of justice cares so much about the poor that he will destroy social structures that tolerate and foster great poverty. He declares he will destroy Israel because of its idolatry and its mistreatment of the poor (Amos 5:11, 6:4, 8:4–6, 9:8). Sodom was destroyed for the same reason. 'She and her daughters were proud because they had plenty to eat and lived in peace and quiet, but they did not take care of the poor and underprivileged. They were proud and stubborn and did the things that I hate, so I destroyed them, as you well know' (Ezek. 16:49–50). There is personal sin and social sin and God holds people responsible for both. If you are a member of a privileged class that profits from structural evil, and do nothing to try and change it, you are guilty before God. The reverse is also true. Martin Luther King wrote: 'To cooperate passively with an unjust system makes the oppressed as evil as the oppressor'.[4]

The second reality is that man is fallen and that the fall affects his personal life, his relationship *and* his institutions. Nothing is free from the effects of the fall. It is not just that institutions, governments, bureaucracies, corporations, clubs and groups are made up of fallen individuals, or that bad personal relationships can spoil worthy intentions: these social institutions have a life of their own that is greater than the sum of their individual members. Round a boardroom table directors can sanction practices that each one would deplore in his private life; in an educational institution administrators can make decisions that are blind to the needs of students and the world; the conflict of unions and management can lead to factories shutting, jobs lost and in sensitive areas of hospitals and fire-services, death. The journalist calls it madness and he is right.

Some discern a theology of such corporate madness in Paul's theology of principalities and powers. These are whatever hinder the progress of God's kingdom in the world: spiritual and demonic forces of rebellion. They find their expression, not only in supernatural form as demons, but in the order that is both necessary to man's life, and corrupts it.

Order is a good creation of God. Respect is due to those who exercise their responsibility for it well. The principalities and powers, which Paul identifies with the State and the law of Israel, are the good creation of God through Christ (Col. 1:16, Rom. 13:1, Col. 2:20–23, Gal. 4:1–11). They are for our good. But order may go wrong. The State and the law can turn oppressive. The good state of Romans 13 can become the oppressive monster of Revelation 13: the law can become an elemental spirit of the universe holding the Jews in bondage. In the name of law and order, the representatives of religion, law and state colluded to murder the God they professed to serve.

This theology of the powers encompasses the ambivalence we find in law and order. Can any current social phenomena be expressed in the language of the powers?

We need some order of morality, some form of justice, some state administration in order to live. But these can be perverted and become tyrannical. An Arab state can execute a girl for marrying a commoner; in the pursuit of profits a food firm can sell dried milk to mothers in Africa and replace nature's purest food factory with expensive powder and infected water; to secure his position of leadership President Amin was able to turn his country into a morgue for his victims. Powerful groups can control politics, economics, the judiciary and education for their own protection and advancement. Justice can become dependent on the ability to pay. These are not individualistic sins. They relate to traditional morality, the laws of the market, the dictates of power, the way of the world we just have to live with if we want to survive. It takes a brave man to stand against them.

Some writers identify Paul's principalities and powers with actual structures; others feel this ignores an important reference to demons. Could we suggest they represent forces which can be expressed both in the demonic possession of people, and the demonic corruption of systems of order in society?

Resisting Social Evil

A biblical analysis of corporate sin, and of the forces man is subject to, injects realism into our social witness. Neutrality is impossible on social issues. If we do and say nothing, our silence leaves the field free for the most powerful. Involvement is essential, if only because the structures cause suffering to millions of individuals. Black South Africans will not attain dignity till apartheid is dead and buried. Understanding is important, for we must know to whom we are talking. International Christians working in cross-cultural situations learn the religious and social background of their neighbours out of courtesy and concern to apply the good news accurately. We cannot address an individual within the structures of Hinduism, casteism, apartheid, council estate, or business management as if he were totally free from the environment which shapes him.

45

His response will reflect the life of his society. The individual is society's child, bound by the forces within that society.

What must we work for? The Bible contains at least four hints. First, repentance is more than an individual matter. When Jonah preached to Nineveh the whole city repented. There is a place for corporate repentance. Second, repentance for complicity in social sin is required. Zaccheus profited enormously from the normal working of the taxation system; and returned most of his profits to the poor. The Bible gives wide scope for the fruits of repentance. We may not alter the system, but can we make reparations to the losers? Our society makes the immigrant feel unwanted, yet for twenty years London Transport and the British National Health Service has depended on immigrant labour. Can we condemn racialism, without showing practical fruits of repentance ourselves? The National Front scorns churchgoers who advocate racial harmony without living in a multi-racial area. At the least we can befriend a Pakistani family.

Thirdly, the complexity of social pressures can make positive help to one group positive harm to another; so how are we to decide which group to help? Landowners in India risk capital by investing in agriculture. Surely they have a right to fix the level of wages they can pay? But if those wages are insufficient to keep a man alive and force him into debt or slavery . . .? Biblical laws such as gleaning-rights, the rights of slaves, and prohibition of excessive interest put the right to justice, food, clothing and the ability to earn a just living above other people's right to manage their property as they like. God is champion of the poor, the most disadvantaged: and so should his servants be.

The fourth hint is God's creation of the church, a new society in which men are freed from the powers of lust, greed, and domination that enslave them and delivered from capitulation to 'the way things are'. They are set in a new environment where the Prince of Shalom rules and where the Spirit creates a new community where people learn to receive and give love. We will develop the importance of the church as God's instrument in society in our next chapter.

The Defeat of Evil

Before men can repent, before they can look to the interests of others, before they can be freed from the powers, before the new society can be formed, evil must be defeated and its power over the world broken. The cross and resurrection of Jesus is the focus of that defeat.

God's programme for the material and spiritual liberation of his creation from the powers of death is to be carried out by a suffering servant. God's love, power and might is supremely revealed not in the order and beauty of the universe, nor in the mountain grandeur or fields of daffodils that adorn many Christian calendars. Go to where the bruises and hurts are in God's creation, a Calcutta bustee, anywhere when people suffer, anywhere when the idea of a good God deserves mockery. Nothing would mock such an idea more than that God's own Son, the agent of his kingdom, could suffer his curse, and be totally abandoned.

We must not isolate Jesus' sufferings from the whole event of his ministry, death and resurrection. They were the birth pangs of the kingdom, the sufferings of the servant appointed to bring God's people under his rule.

His sufferings were *rooted in everyday life*. He lived the life of obedience to God that God's rebellious people refused to give. His crucifixion was the price of his non-conformity, his resistance to injustice among the people of God. His message was the message of the prophets against idolatry and injustice and his fate was the same (Mark 12:1–12).

His sufferings were *the consequence of evil*, a *judgement* upon it. They exposed the Jews' implacable hostility to the real demands of the God of Abraham for repentance, justice and love. What sort of people could they be who crucified the Prince of God's Shalom, their own king? God on a cross indicts the sin of men.

His sufferings were *on behalf of his tormentors*. He had not deserved God's curse. The Messiah died on behalf of

47

his people. He accepted the judgement and death a rebellious people deserve. He died, so they need not die.

His suffering *absorbed the consequences of evil*: the evil of God's enemies. The suffering servant took responsibility for his people's rebellion against God. He was the scapegoat. His suffering was a sacrifice to atone, offered by God as man to God as judge, for the rebellion of his subjects.

It was suffering *motivated by love*. God in Jesus took the initiative in resolving the conflict between a rebellious world and himself and suffered the consequences. He acted as peacemaker, taking the initiative in bringing *shalom*. He loved his enemies.

It was suffering that *dethroned evil*. On the cross Jesus cast out the prince of this world and defeated the principalities and powers. The exact mechanics of the divine-diabolical struggle we are not told, but in the resurrection Jesus emerged victor over the strong man. Evil was bound, its captives could be freed.

All aspects of Jesus' suffering have important theological implications. The cross is the defeat of evil and the price of sin. It frees men from the guilt and power of rebellion against God, setting evil's captives free to be resistance workers. Membership of the kingdom of God is open to his enemies, the price of rebellion has been paid. Those who identify themselves with Jesus under God's curse on the cross find they are now identified with Jesus in the risen life of the kingdom. They are now free from the powers of sin and death to live the life of the new age.

Radical discipleship sees in the cross not only the price of the conquest of evil but also the method. The cross is the centre of history. It is here that the two realities of history meet, the old age and the new, the kingdom of darkness and the kingdom of light. The sufferings of the forerunner of the new age are the very path of victory.

The Fellowship of his sufferings

We must not reduce the cross merely to a contractual necessity in God's task of saving men from sin and isolate it from human suffering. The cross was necessary to God's task precisely because sin, evil and suffering are closely intertwined. The relationship is painted in bold strokes on the biblical canvas. But the lines are never drawn in detail. We must not deprive those who most acutely suffer injustice and pain in God's world from the only message there is of a God who suffers. Redemption from evil comes not through money, education, science, contemplation, meditation or war but through suffering. The cross of Jesus was set up amidst suffering and injustice. It still stands there today. What does it mean?

First, it creates a new race of men free from the power of sin and death. It forms them into a new community where men are free from lust, greed and the desire to dominate others. They reproduce the character of God in loving the poor and the enemy. The lifestyle of the church is to be a witness of the defeat of evil.

Second, the cross speaks of the harsh reality and seriousness of suffering. Suffering is not an illusion, a misfortune, an accident or bad luck. It is the actual result of man's inhumanity to man, for which he is responsible. The suffering of the refugee, the hungry and the unemployed are an indictment of the conquerer, the over-fed and the over-paid. Lazarus sat at Dives' door as an indictment of his indulgence.

Thirdly, the cross speaks of the consequences of standing against injustice and evil, joining the underprivileged against vested interests and taking the initiative in resolving conflict. The one in the middle will be blamed by both sides. The one who exposes the conflict will pay its price. The one who sides with the victims will himself be victimised. Wherever the new age accurately challenges the old, suffering will follow. There will be casualties in the ranks of Jesus' disciples.

Only Christ's sufferings are redemptive. But his sufferings enable his body to resist evil in the world. The sufferings of the Church consolidate the bridgeheads of the kingdom against evil. If the cross and resurrection of Jesus are the kingdom's D-Day, the church's cross is part of the continuing invasion. Suffering authenticated Paul's ministry as an apostle. It was the necessary calling of the whole body of Christ; each part was to take its share of the suffering involved in the mission of God, and the whole body shared in the sufferings of each member. No part was left to suffer alone.

If the church incarnates God's love for the poor and oppressed in standing with them and by resisting injustice, suffering is bound to afflict it. Chris Wigglesworth reflects on the involvement of the western church in helping the Third World:

> Sending money . . . causes problems in the Indian church. It is the personal involvement, the cost of caring for your neighbour which is important. If a large amount of money means you can hire some professionals or you can do the whole thing by remote control, the church in India is spared the pain of working with people.
>
> Now I think making Christ real to people is a painful and costly process and the cost of it for the western church is very often to raise the matter of the whole value system of the west. And this is just the thing the church does not want to do because it threatens our lifestyle and political values. . . .
>
> We should feel the pain of people who have no hope, who have so little joy in life and feel we are their neighbour . . . There has got to be an integrity about all our action so that the way we relate to the immigrant problem, to race relations, is part of our concern of people all over the world. It may be that some time spent with a Pakistani family is a better thing than some money sent to India. The Indian church will take more heart from seeing the church in Britain sweating and being laughed at; it will give the church in India heart to be exposed itself. There's a great deal of partnership in mission, but we tend to look at it very superficially rather than feeling we are bound together in the fellowship of Christ's sufferings.

Fourthly, in Christ all suffering is transformed. The New Testament writings have two responses to suffering. First it is alien to God's world, an intruder to be removed. Jesus never told any sufferer who approached him to endure his suffering. *He healed it*. And he told his followers to relieve suffering whenever they found it – in the sick, hungry, and naked. The motivation is that God's final kingdom has invaded and in that kingdom evil, suffering and injury are to be no more. But sometimes suffering stubbornly remains. Then God defeats it by using it as an instrument of his purpose. The resurrection proclaims that God uses suffering as his instrument of redemption.

We see this dual response in Paul's own experience. When he had a thorn in the flesh, his first response was to ask God to remove it. He prayed in this way three times. The thorn in his flesh still remained. God's answer was: 'My grace is all you need, for my power is strongest when you are weak' (Cor. 12:9). Paul's first and correct response was that the thorn should be removed. When it was not, he discovered a redemptive purpose in it.

Margaret had breast cancer involving painful surgery and radiation. It was a harrowing and anxious time. But somehow her suffering united her family and gave them a deep sense of God's presence. She could not believe God sent the cancer to produce such a result: but rejoiced that God showed his victory over suffering in redeeming it in this way. Is there a similar example from Christian involvement with poverty and injustice? Martin Luther King's Civil Rights Campaign would seem to be the most obvious. Our task in radical discipleship would lead us to discover such redemptive uses of suffering in our own social situation.

Conclusion

Jesus is shown to be Lord over creation by his defeat of evil through suffering and by every defeat of evil in his name. There are many evidences of the cure. The healing of creation is as widespread as the disease. Healing, exorcisms, forgiveness of sin and deliverance from its power shown in good works and fruit of the Spirit are all signs. The use of recalcitrant suffering to further God's purpose of redemption is another sign of Jesus' Lordship. This is not an excuse for leaving victims to their fate, but a policy for intervention in the most hopeless cases. The suffering entailed can only bring us closer to Jesus: 'to experience the power of his resurrection, to share in his sufferings and become like him in his death' (Phil. 3:10); 'Who, then, can separate us from the love of Christ? Can trouble do it, or hardship or persecution or hunger or poverty or danger or death? . . . No, in all these things we have complete victory through him who loved us' (Rom. 8:35–37).

To sufferers God comes with good news – to remove suffering, to take their side, to bring victory out of their suffering. He comes most visibly in his body, the church. The Lordship of Jesus in the New Testament was made visible in a Spirit-filled community which was evidence of a new humanity freed from sin by Jesus, a foretaste of the fulfilment of human life made possible through Jesus, and bearer of the love of God in Jesus for the poor, the outcast and the enemy.

5: The Church
The avant-garde of the New Creation

The evidence that God has raised Jesus and defeated evil is the Christian church. And the only satisfactory explanation of the rise of such a unique human society is the miracle of the Resurrection. Such claims are the unmistakable message of the New Testament. A further staggering one follows – the centre of God's purpose for redeeming human society and the whole cosmos is the Christian church.

What do we mean by the church? We will not use the term to refer to a church building, a local residential congregation, a denomination, or to an invisible membership list of believers, a 'true' church. We will use it, and defend this use at the end of the chapter, to refer to groups of men and women who meet in worship, fellowship and service because they are conscious of their debt to Jesus, to those he loves and what he loves. These groups may be small groups meeting Sunday by Sunday in places of worship, they may be interdenominational action groups, they may be large closely related fellowships of Christian groups in different places. But they are visible, they acknowledge a common Lord and they belong to each other.

The Kingdom Community

What place has the church in the purpose of God? She is the avant-garde of God's new creation. She is where the Lordship of Jesus in the kingdom of God is consciously acknowledged. She is where God's intention for all humanity takes shape in a redeemed community. She is where human relationships are patterned on the kingdom relationships of reconciliation, justice and righteousness. She is where the Spirit of God gives his life and his gifts to produce and sustain a new form of human society. She is a sign of God's new order set in the midst of the old.

As a sign the church points back to the past. As the community of the kingdom where Jesus is Lord she owes her existence to those historical events through which the kingdom invaded. She demonstrates the new relationships of the kingdom, free from the powers of sin and death, and so points to Jesus' defeat of evil, the kingdom pattern of his life, and the coming of his Spirit's powers at Pentecost.

The Church is a sign of the kingdom's presence in the world. God's purpose in Christ is to reconcile all things, to himself and thus to each other. Enmity between man and God, man and man, will be at an end. Jesus made this reconciliation on the cross: so in Christ there is no male or female, Jew or Greek, slave or free. In Christ the racial barrier between Jew and Gentile is shattered. The difference between sexes and races remain, but they are no longer a cause for division, exploitation and bitterness. They are diverse components of God's multi-coloured new creation to be enjoyed with thankfulness.

The church carries on and extends Christ's ministry of reconciliation. She must not tolerate the social divisions of the old order within her membership. Those who claim that they are reconciled to God must be reconciled to each other. Paul insisted that Jewish and Gentile Christians in the Galatian Church accept each other at table fellowship: he instructed rich church members at Corinth whose time was their own to wait till the slaves could come, before starting their communion service; he pleaded that there might be equality in material resources between the churches as he collected for the Jerusalem Church. James demanded that poor people be given the same consideration as anyone else, and that they receive material help.

The church does not always succeed in producing these transformed relationships. The pressures of surrounding society can hinder her. Paul could not abolish slavery on his own. His theology cuts at the root of slavery, and he strongly hinted to Philemon that he should free Onesimus. But his ethical advice is set within the structure of the master-slave relationship. Also the members of the church themselves are prone to live as natural men rather than spiritual men. The Corinthians conformed to the world in their divisions and party spirit. When such things happen, the church is a standing betrayal of the kingdom.

So the church longs for the final deliverance. She is a sign that God's kingdom has invaded but has not arrived in all its fulness. Her celebrations, her worship, her relationships, her communion with her Lord, long for and anticipate the total abandonment of the bride in the arms of the bridegroom.

A Visible Community

A sign must be seen, a candle must be placed on a candlestick, and a city is not set on a hill to be hidden from view. The church is meant to be visible. She is a body, a household, a temple. When people see the church they see the body of Christ, the household of faith and the dwelling of God with men. The traditional division of invisible-visible in the understanding of the church cannot be sustained from the Bible. It too easily lets us off the hook of taking responsibility for the communal life of the visible church.

For the church is a community. God began salvation with Abraham by forming a family, an obedient people. The twelve disciples were symbolic heads of the new people of God. The new life and relationships of the kingdom are to take visible form in a new humanity in Christ. The whole of Paul's ethics of Christian community, and his main ethical guideline, is 'Will this build up the body of Christ?'

The church is a community, not a collection. Her members are not just separate individuals. They depend on each other for life. The Spirit's gifts are to edify other members of the body, members bear one another's burdens, joy to one member brings joy to all. Bodily growth is only possible when each part works properly. The church not only expresses the life of the new order; the life of the church, when working properly, is an actual way into life in the Spirit.

Questions

If this summary approximates to the biblical understanding of the purpose of the church, any Christian church must face specific questions about its life and ministry.

1. Does she regulate her life by obedience to the word of God? If she forsakes Scripture, or denies its relevance to social questions, she abandons the basis for her prophetic calling to declare good news the world needs to hear.

2. Does she see her primary calling to be a sign of the kingdom in the midst of the old order? If she forgets this, her causes, her methods and her life will become captive to the way of the world, however noble her intentions. Her evangelisitic methods, her ways of raising funds, her use of communication media can so often be a poor imitation of worldly salesmanship.

3. Does she incarnate specific values of the kingdom in ways that accurately challenge the values of surrounding society? If the church does not provide alternative structures based on the values of the kingdom, she merely reproduces the divisions of society that disfigure people.

4. Does she seek unity in diversity by deliberately uniting people of different backgrounds, education, social status, income bracket, class and colour into one cohesive body? Is she a multi-racial church in a racialist society? Is she a church of rich and poor in a city? Is she a casteless church in a caste-ridden society? Do her church groups unite young people, parents, single and married? Or do they reproduce the dominant divisions in society? Would she set up a group for unmarried mothers, or would she regard such a proposal as tantamount to advertising a leper colony?

5. Does she provide a community of healing and reconciliation? In their passage through a world infested with personal and social evil people get wounded and personalities get distorted. They build defences, masks and re-

sponses that are designed to defend, retaliate and survive. The church's healing community should provide an environment where wounds are healed, and masks removed: where people can lose the mistrust, suspicion and rejection that this world inculcates and learn to give love by receiving love.

6. Does she seek to discover and draw on gifts from every member? Does she assume that every member is an asset to the whole body or does her way of operating only allow a limited percentage of the membership to contribute? Does she organise herself in a way that encourages each member to discover and exercise a gift?

7. Does her fellowship enable members to commit themselves to each other? Are members available to each other to meet personal and material needs?

8. Do the poor, the uneducated and the rejected find a natural place in the church's community? Does her lifestyle and organisation merely reproduce the structures of the world that injure them? Is her worship and instruction based on literary, abstract, and cerebral methods? Is leadership in all spheres in the hands of those who are successful in life? Does the community as a whole take the side of the victim and the powerless – the gypsy, the immigrant, the unemployed, and the hungry?

9. Does she validate her meetings for worship by presenting herself to God as a living sacrifice which is her logical worship? As the community of the King of Shalom, is she concerned for justice throughout God's creation? Does she seek to serve her Lord in the naked, the hungry and the prisoner? Does she tackle the structural causes of poverty and oppression? Ron Sider notes that the prophets thundered that those who neglect the poor and oppressed are really not God's people at all – no matter how frequent their religious rituals or how orthodox their creeds and confessions, Isa. 1:10–17; 58:3–7. 'The prophetic word against religious hypocrites raises an extremely difficult question. Are the people of God truly God's people if they oppress the poor? Is the church really the church if it does not work to free the oppressed?'[1]

10. Does she structure her fellowship in a way that promotes the values and goals of a kingdom community? Small groups are often best at encouraging mutual commitment. The degree people are committed to a group is in inverse proportion to the size of the group they belong to. Marriage is the most committed relationship of all. Small groups encourage face-to-face relationships, sharing, and caring and enable each member to contribute. Each member can take part in the process of proclaiming the gospel, adding to the congregation, establishing new groups by division, building community, exercising spiritual gifts for upbuilding the group and serving the community outside the church. Howard Snyder contrasts the growth potential in this dynamic model with the limitations of the traditional model, in which a series of concentric circles of fellowship radiate out from the inner core to peripheral individuals.[2] People with more enthusiasm, commitment (and spare time?) can penetrate to the centre. But opportunities for all to participate are severely limited. Some fear that planning for fellowship denies spontaneity and regiments personal relationships. I choose to live with my wife and children in the same house rather than on the other side of town. Am I regimenting love – or expressing it?

These questions drive us to regularly examine our Christian groups to see if their being is denying their message of reconciliation, of wholeness, of healing, of good news to the poor.

When is a church a church?

Radical discipleship means rediscovering that the church is part of the gospel. The being of the visible Christian community is indispensable to its mission. Do the structures of the church serve her mission, or do they deny her gospel? And are there any structures that are essential to make a church a church?

What does make a church a church? The subject is a minefield littered with wrecks of burnt-out inter-denominational arguments on the topic. We can only record two answers given from within the radical discipleship debate.

Jim Punton of the Frontier Youth Trust, and Howard Snyder, favour the view that any Christian group which exercises the *functions* of a church is a church.[3] All structures of the church's *being* are man-made, culturally conditioned, and secondary. They are 'para-church' structures created to serve the functions of a church. The Church of England, Scripture Union, a college Christian Union, the Far East Broadcasting Association and a parish congregation are all equally churches in so far as they exercise church functions. They are equally para-church as structures.

A second view, implicit in the work of Michael Harper[4] and explicit in Ian Cundy's paper 'The Church as Community',[5] stresses that some structural components must demonstrate the identity of a Christian group with the historic community of God's people.

Paul boldly calls the unruly, divided immoral Christians at Corinth 'the church of God which is at Corinth' because he saw this group of baptised Christians as the particular expression there of the total worldwide community of God's people – the Church of God. Therefore each 'local' visible church must express the wholeness of the church of God and continuity with the whole visible church of God. Cundy suggests four criteria, a commitment to the mission of God in lifestyle and service, a commitment to live as a community, a commitment to the total church of God, and a commitment to the apostolic faith.

This relationship between the local church and the total church gives no priority to geographically based congregations over non-residential groups of common interests in claiming the title 'church'. The issue is 'living as a community'. David Clark points out that in our culture there are many other communities of interest apart from those living in the same housing estate.

We may distinguish action groups from co-ordinating groups in distinguishing 'local' from 'total'. It is not the role of a co-ordinating group like the Church of England General Synod to engage as a body in evangelism. That is the role of the action group, the local church. At the same time no action group is free to operate in isolation from any co-ordinating group if it is to be truly a church in continuity with the total community of God's people. Each action group must relate to the wider structures of fellowship, leadership and discipline of the church. 'House-churches' fail to link with such co-ordinating bodies of leadership and discipline. Interdenominational action groups often fail to relate to the right bodies of leadership. They appeal to local churches for support, that is to other action groups. But these local churches are not free agents. They are subject to co-ordinating groups. According to this view the International Council of the Scripture Union should relate to the Methodist conference, the General Synod, and on a world scale to the WCC or WEF.[6] Perhaps it does!

Debate between these views will depend on how far it is possible to separate the *functions* of God's people in the Bible from the *structures* they found themselves in: the structures of nationhood in the Old Testament, and the beginnings of church leadership structures in the New. These expressed membership of one total visible people of God. Can a group be a church without expressing its membership of the total church by relating to a co-ordinating group?

The structure also reinforced the values of the people of God. In Israel the place of the family was heavily reinforced by economic, political and religious structures. In the New Testament the broken barriers of Jew-Gentile, slave-free were reinforced by the existence of only one church of God in Corinth with leadership closely united to the church in Jerusalem. There would have been no place for a white Anglican church existing totally separately from a Black Pentecostal church. The only divisions recognised between churches in the New Testament are geographical, not denominational or doctrinal. And the geographical division is city or province-wide. The dangers of stressing the local 'housing estate' residential group as the being of the church is that it can too easily follow the ghetto-lines of wider society. What values do the structures of our churches reinforce? The New Testament emphasis on the visible unity of the church in each place was a profound outworking of the gospel of free grace that united people across all barriers.

Both views can agree that, given certain conditions, the functions of God's people in mission can be expressed by a church which is not 'local' in the geographical sense. The parish concept only expresses the being of God's people in one cultural setting. In rural England all groups would be represented within the parish boundaries, even though the squire might have a separate pew on Sunday. As our cities divide into ghettos of white-collar paleface suburbanites and blue-collar multi-coloured inner city dwellers, could the being of the church be better expressed in cross-cultural churches spanning residential areas, or by very close links between churches in different areas?

We must continually work away at the structures of the visible church so that they are faithful to the being of the church as a multi-racial one-caste participating society; not only considered as a world-wide totality, but in each local expression.

6: God and society

Evangelical Christians often argue that since only the Christian Church (or parts of it) knows the gospel, its duty is to verbalise the good news; other people can care for the city's drains.

Radical discipleship seriously questions this division of labour. For one thing the good news must been seen in flesh, so the church must be a faithful *expression* of the good news. Secondly, any compassionate evangelism among eighty per cent of the world's population runs into problems of lack of bread and employment. With twenty per cent of our world the problem is one of too much bread. Thirdly this division assumes that atheist non-Christians will know perfectly well how to look after the city's drains. Among Protestant atheists in England this may be true. In other cultures the law of the old order is more pronounced. The wealthy and influential get drains – the rest don't.

But there is no need to urge Christians to get involved in society. Christians are involved in society anyway – through their jobs, their housing, their choice of consumer goods, their use of educational and medical facilities, the way they run their cars and their savings. The problem is that they are given little idea of how to be involved Christianly, apart from being honest and hard-working. They are therefore subject to every pressure from the social order to conform and to follow the dominant ideology of society.

Community and Involvement

The enthusiasm for a Christian community and the fellowship of the church that forms part of radical discipleship must not be mistaken for a monastic retreat from involvement. Christian community is essential for Christian involvement in society. Changes in our way of life then alter our basic securities and challenge the conventional wisdom of our peer groups. The Christian community should provide the security that enables us to sit loose to the things usually regarded as essential for security. For example in India unemployed graduates generally consider manual work beneath their dignity and qualifications. Christians are not exempt from this feeling. Will the Christian community give those members who take manual jobs the psychological security of feeling they are doing a dignified and worthwhile job – or will they look down on them, with the rest of society?

What is the relationship between preaching the gospel and Christian involvement in society? We can trace the relationship through many theological themes. We can begin with salvation. 'Salvation means repentance, submitting to Jesus, and entering the new community of Jesus' disciples where all relationships including economic relationships are being redeemed.'[1] Salvation is possible because the kingdom of God has come and has won. Right relationships in the kingdom of God are patterned on the life of the people of God in the Scriptures. Here we find no dichotomy between attitude and action, concern for man's spirit and concern for his body, spiritual salvation and material deliverance. We find that action for the poor is the acid test of the reality of our faith in Jesus, of our salvation.

As the community of the kingdom seeks for right relationships among its members it will be drawn to seek those right relationships in wider society. When people enter the kingdom they repent, both of personal sin and of involvement in social sin. But such repentance should eventually mean seeking to change the social structures themselves. A Christian businessman in Bangalore, South India, had a good personal reputation for honesty and for never taking or giving bribes. He went bankrupt. His integrity was intact but he could not gather other traders who were sympathetic to honest dealings, and work with them for honesty.

When people live the life of the kingdom in the community of the kingdom they should discover important values in human life, for example that people matter more than things, that women are not to be the sexual playthings of men, that each person has a gift to contribute to his society. Hopefully people will learn how human beings should treat each other and will wish to extend their knowledge to widen society. For example Christians have a strong understanding of human sex relations out of concern to 'preserve family life' and so have waged war against pornography, blue films and obscenity on television.

The concern has been two-fold. First Christians cannot bring up their families in isolation from the influences of wider society. So they want to ensure that the standards of wider society reinforce rather than undermine Christian values. This concern is inward looking and perfectly defensible. But secondly Christians also know the blessing of family life and wish to preserve its values in wider society for the good of their fellow men.

But this reasoning should go further. Family life is not only affected by pornography and blue films. Shift work, unsocial working hours, housing conditions, and lack of playspace for children also affect family life. Structures of employment and housing bring great strains. Are Christians as concerned about those? The Old Testament has a great concern not only for the family but also for the economic structure of land tenure to prevent pauperisation of families, and the social structures of the tribe and nation to give a family a wider sense of belonging.

Through the work of the gospel in creating Christian community, Christians learn human values. The structures in society around it affect the degree to which the community can put these values into practice. So Paul could not abolish slavery himself, though his theology and personal advice undermines the whole system. As the community learns these human values it will seek to change the social structures as far as possible so that they promote rather than negate them. Good social structures will not save men, but bad ones will destroy much that makes human life human. Christians, who experience God's redeemed human life, will work for any cause in society that embodies the meaning of God's redemption of human life in Christ.

As Christians work for God's values throughout society they proclaim the lordship of Christ in deed. As we work to embody the meaning of God's salvation in every aspect of life men will see what we mean by the good news of God's deliverance. 'Sometimes precisely the act of working in the name of Jesus for improved socio-economic conditions for the oppressed enables persons to understand the proclaimed word of God's love in Christ.'[2] The word of God in Christ is that Jesus, the King of righteousness is Lord: that God's kingdom of right relationships is the goal of human history and the plumbline for human society. God's concerns are for justice, especially for the poor and oppressed. If we acknowledge the Lordship of Jesus over all, we will seek to eradicate those things that deny his Lordship and will seek to embody those concerns that express his Lordship.

Understanding Peoples' Needs

The witness of the church in society is to demonstrate the dynamic lordship of Jesus. This entails hard work in understanding our situations so that we can declare that Lordship with relevance. We must address the actual needs and issues that people are struggling with.

We must listen to the real needs of people. In India during the emergency (1975–77) thousands of poor people, including poor Christians, were dragged off buses to be sterilised. But the leaders and middle class members of the Indian church said nothing. They were not being sterilised – they merely appreciated the fact that the trains ran on time. They were not listening to the cries of others.

In the west there is a great need to understand the real nature of poverty in India. Poverty is not an economic matter. The great majority of studies show that economic aid only benefits the wealthy classes because money gravitates to those who already possess it. Poverty is linked with the social fabric. People are kept poor by the patterns of ownership and of land, by political power, and by the caste system which places a religious sanction against poorer classes ever improving themselves. What poor people need is a value system that gives them a sense of self-worth and dignity. They need the encouragement to unite together and stand for their rights. The right to work, a fair wage and minimal housing which are all guaranteed in India's Constitution.

In Britain also, radical evangelical Christians draw attention to the need to understand the social context of peoples' problem. Roger Sainsbury writes:

> I believe Jesus wants his disciples to be those who question the society in which they live and turn this questioning into caring and action. It is increasingly being seen that *youth work cannot be done in isolation from community activity*. Our youth work must be related to work in the community and if we really care for young people we must work through community development processes to change the society in which the young people live.[3]

Robert Holman writes as the conclusion to his study on Poverty:

> Whatever the means of instigating change those who advocate a more equal society are sometimes charged with paying too much attention to material matters, of regarding possession as more important than people. The opposite is true. It is realised that the quality of peoples' relationships underlies a satisfactory life . . . Most people seek mutually satisfying contacts with others. Yet these relationships cannot be entirely separated from material matters. Concern, love, compassion, feelings, must be expressed through the sharing of resources . . . When great disparities occur, then not only are distress and disadvantage created but so are behaviour patterns which can lead to apathy, extreme aggression and the inability to survive in modern society. In short, grossly unequal conditions are likely to promote those features which inhibit the growth of happy relationships. I believe in seeking those structural changes

which will lead to a society in which the distribution of resources will facilitate concern for others, tolerance and sharing.[4]

The Church and Politics

This means we cannot reduce all problems to the micro-problems of individuals. It means that the church as the church, and not just as Christian citizens, must be involved in politics. Charles Elliot's essay in *Christian Faith and Political Hopes*, according to fellow-contributor Haddon Willmer, defines politics as the choosing between possible human relationships; and (as we have noted) Ron McMullen states 'A political act is one whereby there is an effort to preserve or change what exists in social structures.' The church cannot be neutral in politics, however hard it tries. Its business is human relationships. Even by its non-involvement it supports the status quo of relationships between those with and those without power.

In the 1979 American oil crisis, a Christian economist Dr. Norman Ewert of Wheaton College, Illinois commented in a BBC interview that the Mennonite and Episcopal Churches in the USA had said and done nothing about the Government's unwillingness to limit petrol usage because they were profiting from agricultural and real estate investment; they were part of the system whereby United States' citizens pay, at the time of writing, one third of the price for their petrol that citizens of India pay. On whose side is the American church standing?

Paul is usually cited as witness for the view that the church should be politically silent. But his words in Romans 13 would encourage the church that it has a duty to show to the State or the magistrate the good which it is their God-given task to reward. Does the magistrate have some knowledge of God's will for a just society independent of God's revelation? No. It is the church's duty by its teaching and practice to show God's standards. When the magistrate begins to reward evil and punish good, the church should clearly show where the good lies. On this understanding of Paul, Martin Luther King based his practice of civil disobedience in the face of legalised segregation in the Southern United States.

Men of Good Will

So the church must be involved in seeking God's right relationships and justice in the whole of society. Does it undertake this task alone? If God's will for his redeemed world is that the hungry shall be fed, are none of those working to feed the hungry doing part of the work of God's kingdom except Christians? We cannot resort to calling people of good-will anonymous Christians. People rightly resent that sort of Christian imperialism. We do not have to decide whether people of good will who are also concerned for justice are Christians. We can gratefully acknowledge that every good and perfect gift comes from above (James 1:17), and Paul encourages us to fill our minds with things that are good and deserve praise, things that are true, noble, right, pure, lovely and honourable (Phil. 4:8). Wherever we see truth overcoming error and right overcoming wrong, we see God's will being done.

Of course there is more to be done. Of course it is not possible to have God's kingdom of right relationships in society in its fullness without men giving their allegiance to God's King. And of course the full expression of God's kingdom will not come till Jesus returns. But if God is at work now in the world for his will to be done, we can rejoice to see fragmentary expressions of his will the world over. For example three years of living in a country with minimal health services for the majority have taught me that the British National Health Service – for all its failings – is somewhat nearer a just and fair method of providing health care for all than the system in India.

But how do we tell where God's will is being done, if it is not being done by believers? The patterns for God's will given in the Scriptures are our guide. How do we work with those who have a concern for truth and justice and society? We have no blueprint for Utopia, no infallible plan for the kingdom of heaven. Therefore we are free to join, for limited action, with those who share common concerns.

We do not have to reach unanimity on every point of ideology before uniting for common action.

So in March 1978 a Race March in Leeds protesting against the prejudices of the National Front was peopled by members of the Gay Liberation Front, the Communist Party and Leeds churches. In the relief operations after the Andhra Pradesh cyclone in November 1977, Christians found themselves working alongside militant Hindus.

If Christians do not join in the hard and laborious task of working for just relationships in society, what right have they to criticise the results of other mens' attempts to organise political or social life? They deserve the rebuke delivered by an author to a reviewer of his book: 'Where were you when the pages were blank?'

This means we must widen our concept of Christian work. Our church work must go beyond supporting the activities of Christian fellowships. Membership of trades unions or tenants' associations counts in my book as Christian work. In Bangalore, a city where over 300 people are killed on the road a year, Christian work would involve teaching road safety in schools or tightening up traffic regulations. In the West so much of everyday life is imbued with Christian values that we take a lot for granted and narrow Christian concerns to what happens *inside* men rather than what takes place *between* them.

Often it is non-Christians who teach the church what God's will in society is. God uses non-Christians as a judgement on the church and a stimulus for it to act. The activities of Oxfam and other agencies pricked some Christian consciences into starting Tear Fund. Many evangelicals refused to contribute to Oxfam because it was not Christian. But they were using this as an excuse for not contributing to relief work through any other agency either. Therefore an evangelical relief agency was started.

When Kingdom-shaped things happen, whoever does them and however insignificant they are, God's kingdom is at work. As Christians we are to work to establish God's kingdom and as full members of kingdom communities demonstrate our membership by living its values. If we do so, then the church may indeed become a home for those who seek wholeness and who want to take a stand for social justice. We must ask where those who want to seek a secure foundation and motivation for a just and human society will ever find their rest. Is not Jesus the source and goal of a true humanity, the true image of God? Vinay Samuel writes of a gifted and talented Sikh engineer who

> came back to serve India after training and service in California. He swapped a magnificent lifestyle for a pumping station hut. In the two years he spent in India he watched Christian groups and read the Scriptures. At the beginning of 1980 he came to the conclusion that the only inspiration, motivation and sustaining power for justice and development in India lay in Jesus Christ. He discovered that in seeking the basis and motivation and power for a social stand for justice, Jesus was the only religious leader whom he discovered in front of him, calling 'Follow me.'
>
> Our dream is that the church can and should become the home of a radical Christian understanding of humanity, justice and social development. . . . Within the church they will then discover the human, spiritual and divine resources for them as individuals and groups to go out and change India. The church will produce such people. We dare to think it could also be a home for people with similar social concerns for social justice as marked Jesus' stance, but who are yet unable to accept the total Christian world-view. While we would rejoice if the church were to become a home for such 'men of good will', we do not suggest that the church should include as full members people who do not acknowledge Jesus as Lord.[5]

A Model or an Instrument of Change?

To be such a home for wholeness, the church in its own structures must be the model of the humanity and justice that it professes. This is the truth emphasised by those who stress the role of the church as a model to society. But the pattern for the church's mission is the pattern of the incarnation. Jesus sent the disciples into the world 'as the Father sent me' (John 20:21). Jesus did not only demonstrate the life of righteousness; he was involved in the history of the world, to bring God's righteousness by defeating the strong man of evil and inaugurating the new era of God's kingdom.

Between the close of the prophetic age and the advent of Jesus, the Jews assumed that God was no longer active in his world to defeat evil and bring righteousness. Jesus came as Emmanuel, God at work among us, as Jesus who will save men from the prison and the consequences of their sins, to bind the strong man of evil and set his captives free now. It is not sufficient for the church to provide a model to the world of how it should be. It must be actively involved in the historical process to enable human society become as far as possible what God wills it to be, now. The church must actively grapple with evil men and evil powers both by prayer and by calling men to repent, and by working for justice and change where the work of evil is defacing the image of God in men. The church must declare the good news of the kingdom and convict men of sin in the power of the Spirit by working for those relationships in society which speak of God's justice, which demonstrate Jesus' Lordship, and which promote the dignity and equality of men created in the image of God. She must show the need to acknowledge Jesus as Lord by demonstrating that he is the source and the power for the right relationships of the kingdom. She must witness to God's judgement and grace not in word only, but in action identifying and seeking to redeem relationships that speak of injustice, sin and rebellion against God both between individuals and in more complex social relationships.

In Bangalore there are many small businesses which employ non-union labour. These businesses are as exploitative as the Victorian sweatshops against which Lord Shaftesbury campaigned. A small gathering of Christians in industry in Bangalore agreed on the vital need to provide a centre to give legal aid and advice to these exploited workers, to enable them to gain the rights which belong to them under the labour laws, but which their employers flout with impunity. To bring right relationships for these exploited workers, Christians must not only model just employment practices in their own organisations (and they are not always

71

known for doing that), they must be involved in the historical process of enabling those practices to obtain for the powerless.

Blind Pessimism

Many Christians would urge at this point in the argument that the record of history is that the involvement of the church has made no difference to halting the progress of evil in the world. If anything the world gets worse every day. Hendrik Berkhof describes this view in these words:

> The average Christian does not expect to see any positive signs of Christ's reign in the world. He believes that the world only becomes worse and races in the direction of the antichrist. He has a feeling that God looks on, powerless, and that God will have his chance in the far future through a sudden interference. The average Christian is not aware of the presence of the Kingdom in the world today. But he is prepared to believe in the presence of Christ in his personal life, in prosperity as well as adversity. It is sometimes very moving to see how strong this faith can be, even and particularly in the darkest hours. But it is depressing to see how helpless and fearful this same Christian often is when he reads his newspaper or when he thinks about his children's future.[6]

Such a pessimistic view is blind to the signs of Christ's reign in the present. Berkhof describes them as follows:

> The Lord who makes his entrance into the world through the missionary proclamation is the Redeemer who comes to seek and save what is lost. He comes not to be served, but to serve. . . . And the man who through the proclamation is called to freedom begins to reflect some of these divine attributes in his humility, consciousness of guilt, self-denial, and readiness to forgive and serve. Thus, a new idea of *being human* is ushered in; it is not the proud humanity of the Greeks, but the humanity of humility. Particular attention is given to the suffering and oppressed. An ordinary street scene, such as an ambulance stopping all traffic because *one* wounded man must be transported, is the result of the coming of the Kingdom . . . All this is against the natural 'life-concepts' of man dominated by the powers of nature. Ideas such as responsibility, humility, consciousness of guilt, service, etc., create a gulf between what

man ought to be and what he is. A deep *awareness of norms* is developed, coupled with a *dissatisfaction* with the existing world, which can no longer be appreciated as the expression of the divine will. They begin to resist whatever does not conform to the norms. The battle is pitted against exploitation, injustice, and slavery, and against everything that is not motivated by love. The idea of social justice so well-known to us was injected by the missionary proclamation. We believe that although this justice does not eliminate the differences among men, it does lessen them.[7]

Berkhof notes that as a result of the missionary endeavour, 'a whole nation gratefully eats of the fruit, but only a minority desires the tree which produces the fruit. Many try to forget or deny from which tree these fruits are derived. They make the fruit an end in itself.'[8]

So the changes that the kingdom brings always contain the possibility of the demonic if they are not related to Christ. We also find in the Scriptures that as the kingdom advances, the forces of antichrist and evil become more virulent in opposition as they see the notice of their defeat written and their hour of banishment approach. They even use and counterfeit the gifts of God. So we should not be surprised to see that science gives us both medicines to cure disease, and nuclear bombs to wipe out the human race. The coming of the kingdom unleashes both the power of God and the resistance of evil as Satan sees his goods being despoiled. So when the pessimistic Christian sees the spread of evil, he is selectively reading the evidence, and takes for granted the good things of life which are fruits of God's kingdom. The challenge is not to throw up our hands in fatalistic despair, or to buy ourselves out of the problems of life in personal retreat, but to seek the power of God to storm Satan's next stronghold so that God's peace and justice may prevail over a wider area.

In the following pages I gather a number of suggestions about practical ways in which we can express the lifestyle of the kingdom of God. Of all our actions and practices we must ask if they reflect the values and concerns of God's kingdom in the manner that God's kingdom works. Does what we do, or condone, bring justice for the poorest people? And does it uphold the value of persons above things?

7: The Church
The discipleship training centre

So far in this book I have tried to outline the biblical foundations for what is known as radical discipleship. But my chief purpose is to act as a catalyst to translate these concerns into the everyday teaching and fellowship programmes of churches, youth groups and camp programmes. For many years there has been an accepted systematic theology of what to teach and when in Christian training programmes. I quote the chapter readings from the Scripture Union manual, *The Way* by Geoffrey Robinson and Stephen Winward: 'The Christian Life', 'How to Pray', 'How to Read the Bible', 'How to Live a Disciplined Life', 'How to Deal with Temptation', 'How to Receive Divine Guidance', 'How to Live in Fellowship', 'How to Serve God', 'How to Win Others'.

Not a word of *The Way* needs rewriting. It has priceless lessons tried and tested by experience. But it was printed first in 1945 and revised in 1961. In the past thirty-five years the Christian community has learnt much about biblical obedience due to the solid foundations laid by authors like Robinson and Winward. Our best tribute to their foundation is to build on it. Our study of the theology of radical discipleship raises a number of questions about evangelism and teaching in the Church.

A Personal Relationship of Discipleship

Our aim in evangelism is not to win converts but to produce disciples – to produce Christians who have a lively relationship with Jesus expressed in commitment to Christian fellowship, and in witness and service to the world's social and spiritual needs. What we must be clear about in our evangelism is the nature of the relationship into which Jesus calls men.

The personal relationship with Jesus which evangelists speak of is discipleship.

How early in a Christian's life should we raise issues of discipleship? Jesus' answer was, 'before it begins'. He made the challenge of discipleship very clear to the rich young ruler. He began by meeting his felt needs. The rich young ruler wanted eternal life and Jesus answered his questions. But Jesus went beyond his felt need to challenge him at the point of relevant obedience: give your wealth to the poor and follow me. Jesus described his relationship to the young man, not as one who met his felt needs and would leave more uncomfortable issues till later, but as one who was his Lord, right at the outset of what could have been his Christian life.

Our aim in evangelism is to present Jesus as the one who calls men to discipleship. If we only present him to people as one who meets what they feel their needs to be at the time, we can distort Jesus. We fail to present him as the one who challenges and has the power to transform every aspect of life. If we wait till people are 'mature' before they meet the full-blooded Jesus, we may find they have already answered many questions of Christian discipleship with no reference to the real Jesus at all, but only to the one imprisoned in their own felt needs.

Jesus was unique in his time in calling people to discipleship. Jewish students asked permission to attach themselves to a rabbi as his disciples, and bound themselves to the law. Jesus took the initiative in calling men *and women* to discipleship, and called them to follow him.

Jesus' call 'Follow me' was not a call just to enjoy personal friendship with him in private. It was a call to follow him in the public stance he took in Palestinian society, to join his community which broke social barriers, flouted Jewish laws, and renounced the values of leadership by domination; to eat with social outcasts, fraternise with Samaritans, heal the sick, take the side of the poor, be prepared to appear in court before kings and governors and risk the cross.

Discipleship covers every aspect of a person's life. It is not just a religious relationship for being right with God. When we come to Jesus we enlist as subjects of the Lord of the whole of life as it should be and will be. Therefore repentance for rebellion against him, forgiveness and a new relationship with him, receiving his Spirit and being committed to Jesus and his people cover every aspect of life. When Zacchaeus repented, he made reparations to those he had cheated. When the disciples were filled with the Spirit they shared their possessions. We are committed to live as servants of the Lord of things as they should be. If we are in a right relationship with him we should want to see his right relationships prevail in human relationships.

If we are forgiven by him we must forgive others (Matt. 18:35). If we have saving faith we will take action to ensure that the hungry and naked have the necessities of life. If we want to serve him we will feed and clothe his poor hungry and naked brothers (Matt. 25:40). We will devote our time, energy, skills and effort not to assuring ourselves of the basic necessities of life but to seeking his kingdom and right relationships in our part of the world (Matt. 6:33). The reality of our claim to be in the right with God will be seen in our relationships in the family, in employment, with children, with the poor and with our enemies.

Obedience in the Face of Rebellion

These new relationships empowered by God's spirit will express our obedience to our Lord. The actions which express Christian obedience will change from generation to generation. Rebellion against God takes different forms in different ages and areas.

No one in England today would doubt that electoral bribery would be inappropriate for a Christian and therefore for anyone else. But the celebrated evangelical William Wilberforce indulged in what we would now call electoral bribery as many men of otherwise high principle do in some countries today. It was and is just the system in many places. In Wilberforce's day, as in India today Christian obedience which really counted would be to refuse electoral bribery. And indeed Wilberforce came to renounce any opportunity he might have had to gain advantages by obtaining favourable jobs for his supporters. To define Christian obedience in England 1981 as the refusal to countenance electoral bribery would be to state the boringly obvious. But to use such a definition in some other countries today would be most relevant.

Paul defined Christian obedience for the Galatian church as the willingness for Jewish Christians to eat with Gentile Christians. No Jewish Christian would now refuse to eat with a non-Jewish Christian. The issue is dead. But in India many high-caste Indian Christians will not attend the same church as their low-caste Christian brethren. And in South Africa men have institutionalised racial separation in the name of Christianity.

Our obedience to God's word interprets the meaning of the Bible to the world today. If the Bible says 'All are one in Christ Jesus,' and the world sees black Christians in Leeds cold-shouldered out of white churches so that they have to form their own, then the world knows that 'All are one in Christ Jesus' means 'All white men are one in Christ Jesus'.

We must see how the standards of the kingdom of God identified the crucial areas of rebellion in the societies of biblical times. We must then use these standards to identify rebellion against God – worldliness – today. Current examples of worldliness in the West are the pursuit of material values above personal values and the competition in western schools, business and even some Christian organisations. In India worldliness is at present the pursuit of wealth, power and status and the practice of bribery and corruption in education, business and the civil service. Christians are not free from this. One head of a Christian institution gave instructions that if necessary a bribe should be paid for land purchase.

Obedience is not legalism. Legalism is a static concern with forms of obedience which may have been important once, but are now irrelevant or trivial. For example, in parts of India, Christians condemn cinema-going as a worldly sin. The history of this is that Christians in the American South frowned on theatres, dances and cinemas because they promoted licentiousness. They identified renunciation of these leisure pursuits as essential to the Christian life. Then their missionaries transported this obedience to India. In India, 200 million people attend cinemas each week and sex relationships are rigidly controlled and certainly not endangered in cinemas. By condemning the cinema Christians lose a common ground with most of the population. But worse, they focus attention on cinema-going as an example of sin and never mention the bribes they may have paid or the rock bottom wages they pay their domestic servants. Legalism is yesterdays' obedience: it blinds us to the crucial issues of today. The content of worldliness and biblical obedience must change from generation to generation.

Holiness

When we teach men to obey the Lord, we will be teaching them to be holy. To be holy means to be separated from ordinary use, set aside for God's use. It means being ready to be used as God desires, to express his concerns. What are God's concerns? For example, they are that justice should be done to the poor and oppressed, that men should seek their security not in wealth but in God's provision and should share their resources with the poor. God's people do not demonstrate their holiness if they remove themselves from difficult and compromising situations of life into the realm of unquestionable purity. This is what the Pharisees did. They were the 'separate' ones. Their idea of holiness was of ritual and behavioural purity. A Pharisee was shocked that Jesus did not immediately dissociate himself from a woman of the streets. Jesus had a different concept of purity altogether – purity of heart which could enter into any impure situation. We demonstrate our holiness as we are channels of God's action to fulfil his concerns.

As we discuss old terms with their biblical meanings, we see how Christianity differs from religion. The transforming life of Christ, available to the believer, distinguishes the gospel from religion. In many religions salvation is escape – escape from the harsh realities of social, political and material life. In Christianity, salvation is not such a way out. For Jesus creates new men within reality, and through them, transforms reality. God had a purpose in creating the world; and as men turn to the Lord of creation as it should be, they join themselves to the rolling plan through which God is bringing his original purpose to completion. This is achieved not by religious practices but by the transformation of the everyday realities of life.

Discipleship training needs to concentrate far more on relating biblical patterns and imperatives for obedience and holiness to how we earn our money, the motives behind our education, where we live, what size car we own and what use we make of it, the part we play in community life, what we expect of friends, how we furnish our home and the contact we have with under-privileged people.

We will not deliver legalistic answers any more than Jesus did. But we will give a model for raising important questions such as: 'How far does what I do show that I belong to the Bride of a carpenter in Nazareth?' 'How much of my energy and time is taken up with demonstrating that God is on the side of the poor?' 'How far is the life of the community of Christians I belong to a force for achieving biblical social justice in our area?'

The Place of the Personal

Some may fear that an emphasis which I feel restores to evangelical faith a biblical balance for social justice, in fact submerges the (essentially personal) relationship between believers and a personal God, which is the rationale behind the meaning of persons. On the contrary: the emphasis on the personal is very good news in the social sphere. To millions of oppressed people the gospel is good news, telling them that they have a dignity and personal worth totally denied to them by the system. In the West they may be dehumanised by computers, mass production or 'Big Brother'; in the East, by caste oppression and economic slavery. The gospel tells those labourers in India who are bound to serve their creditors for life in order to pay off a debt of twenty pounds, that they are sons of God; that they should not be treated like that. It gives them confidence to stand up for their rights. Among oppressed people there is a tragic circle. Because they are treated like animals by superior groups they can only attain a feeling of status by treating others below them in the same way. The gospel frees people from needing to lord it over others to establish their status and identity.

The only way of preserving the fruits of any change in structures is to have transformed persons. We need both transformed structures and new people. Otherwise selfish people will use new structures for their own ends. And a change in people is a part of the revolution that is needed. Sebastian Kappen, a Christian Marxist in India, writes that the goal of revolution is not just a change in the social system. Its goal is the creation of a new man, a new consciousness, a new sensitiveness to values and a new vision of the world. A new consciousness is necessary, for how will selfishness beget concern for others, hatred beget love, competition beget co-operation? The growth of such a consciousness is not just a means to promote structural change, but a partial realisation of the revolution itself.[1]

The following example shows the need for both social and personal change. One major development project in India brought relief to a Christian village which had been devastated by a natural disaster. It also opened up new employment opportunities for them. But an evaluation two years later showed that as in many similar projects the community had not yet been instilled with a spirit of servanthood, of moving from their new found security to meet the needs of others.

Christian servanthood, according to Vinay Samuel, is:

The unlimited availability of all resources and skills to enable especially the poor to be fulfilled. This stance, in our present day, is at variance with the concern to bring all down to one level and make the scientist a sweeper: it is at variance with the concern to give equal opportunity to all to better themselves independently of the community: it is at variance with the notion that those endowed with greater skills should enjoy more of the resources of a community. It is the concern that all should have the opportunity to be servants, to find fulfilment in enabling all to find fulfilment.[2]

To enable people to live as servants in this way, both new people and also new structures are needed, which will facilitate rather than hinder (though they will never automatically produce) Christian servanthood. There is no need to put personal and social change as two extremes, two opposites which can never be reconciled. Both are vitally necessary.

The Power of the Spirit

For a Christian community to be socially relevant it must be empowered by God's Spirit. For the Spirit is the only agent who can produce in men the desire to seek and the will to obey the agenda for the life of God's kingdom. God's kingdom and its right relationships cannot be lived or achieved by unaided human effort or by the methods of the fallen world.

The Spirit produces the new man needed for God's plan for society. All discussions of the values and attitudes necessary for any change in society must include discussions of changing self-centred people into people who are not only concerned for others but are willing to suffer deprivation and loss themselves, so that others might gain a fuller life. This pattern of life, of dying to oneself that others might live, is the pattern of Jesus which only the Spirit of Jesus can reproduce in men. This pattern is very necessary today. Christian development workers in India stress how it is vitally necessary for skilled educated Christian people to identify with the illiterate hungry people to work with them for justice and change. Economists stress that worldwide economic justice will only come when rich nations experience the pain of giving up wealth and advantages so that poor nations can advance.

The Spirit gives the gifts which the Christian community needs to live the life of the kingdom. Charismatic gifts should not be thought inessential to Christian social justice. For the Christian community to witness to the reality of God's kingdom, to be agents of its life in society and tangible evidence of its reality, it needs all the Spirit's gifts for its community life.

The Life of the Community

Intense pressure surrounds new believers and old to abandon biblical models; norms of obedience in the social sphere favour contemporary values. Believers can only sustain a deviant lifestyle as they strengthen and support each other. There is a continuing need to discover various different forms of Christian community which can give such support. It simply is not on to expect all Christians to move into shared households. There must be experiments in sustaining community life in Christian fellowships.

Many discipleship training courses concentrate on 'the means of grace' – prayer, Bible study and personal moral change in overcoming temptation and finding God's will. These have tended to concentrate on individuals. Would we be more faithful to biblical discipleship and more adequate to the challenges of discipleship if we taught the whole pattern of biblical obedience? This pattern would include God's standards for personal life and justice in society: God's provision of new life and the power of the Spirit: and God's plan of an obedient supportive community. This pattern of obedient discipleship should be demonstrated to new believers in the ongoing life of a Christian community. In the community of Christ's people we are to learn to love in a Christlike way as we receive Christlike love. Church life should itself be a discipleship training course.

8: Love and people

Much Christian preaching is genuinely beautiful. It speaks of a new force in human affairs, the self-giving love of God who became a poor man and gave his life for undeserving enemies. God's kingdom brings this pattern for relationships into men's lives. These new relationships are not innate in men. They need to be learnt. But there is no blueprint for them. They are a matter of attitude, style and commitment.

When men and women respond to God's unconventional love, do we teach them how to receive and give love like this? Or are we in danger of loading them with rules? Do we speak too soon about do's and don'ts for maintaining a Christian life, before people begin to *enjoy* this love? There is no dichotomy between love and maintaining a Christian life. The basis for both is our relationship with Jesus and how that relationship is expressed in all our relationships. But sometimes we crowd love out with advice and rules which become legalism.

Could we not begin our discipleship training with teaching on love? Christianity is about the love of God and love for people on behalf of God. When people respond to Jesus, God's love is poured into their hearts through his Spirit and flows out to others. How can we help new Christians relate to others in a truly loving way? We cannot assume that they know.

We can help people learn to forgive and accept themselves and others. Jesus teaches that this is to be the first result of God's forgiveness. As people face the pain and difficulties of forgiving another person, they learn what it means for God to forgive them. They also prove that they are grateful to God for forgiving them. They begin to link their new relationship with God to new relationships with others. Could we ask members of a beginners' group to make a private list: 'Who can't I accept? Who can't I forgive?'? Without referring to personalities they could perhaps discuss why they find forgiveness difficult. A group in our church in Bangalore gave us an answer. 'If I forgive someone, he will think I am weak and will take advantage of me in future.' In this way people can learn how vulnerable God's love is. We will also discover resentments and fears for Christ's love to heal.

New Christians have a mission field among their families, close friends, old acquaintances and enemies. How could they learn to comfort them with the love by which they are comforted by God? (2 Cor. 1:4). Can our discipleship training teach them empathy, and train them to be 'good listeners'? They need not wait until they have stock Christian answers to the problems of life. Morgan Derham writes:

> It is agreed by church growth experts that a Christian has the greatest potential as an evangelist in the three months immediately following his conversion (before he has had time to attend a school of evangelism), because he still understands the way non-Christians think and feel and so can communicate more easily with them.[1]

We need to expose new Christians to this new quality of love so that they can share it with others: this would include anticipating another's needs, being available for people, sharing our possessions and our very selves. A Christian couple, newly converted and recently married, told a sharing group with obvious delight how they moved into their new home and found the food cupboard full. An hour or so later, a freshly made meal was delivered to their door by members of their church. We shouldn't be surprised if they arrange such surprises for others in turn.

We do not learn this new kind of love by being told about it. We must experience it from the Christian community and learn to express it ourselves. The church must be the training ground. The whole of a local church must feel itself involved in training new disciples. Discipleship training courses run by parachurch organisations divorced from the life of the local church cannot provide this essential dimension. If the church is to be the learning ground for these new relationships, we must help the church community to practice them. This will inevitably drive us back to the Scriptures to find the pattern of these relationships. It will drive us forward to interpret authentically what the Scriptures require of us in today's situations.

Love and Poor People

Discipleship training must cover the biblical teaching on working for justice for the under privileged. The people to whom God gives priority are the poorest. Therefore the poorest have the prior claim on the Church's attention, energy and resources. We examined the Bible's teaching on the poor in Chapter 3. I am not concerned to argue for or against capitalism or socialism. I *do* want to discover principles for our behaviour in relation to world poverty.

Our political action, our simple lifestyle or our dedication to a specific ministry must be biblically and theologically informed.

Three principles from Scripture should inform our behaviour in this area. First, the right of human beings to have the basic necessities of life takes priority over the rights of property owners to enjoy exclusive unfettered use of their resources. What we own is not private property. The parable of the talents teaches us that resources are held in trust for the good of the community. They are not for exclusive unquestioned private enjoyment. The person with ten talents did not receive ten more talents to keep. He was given responsibility for ten cities. Donald Hay outlines a Christian decision on these lines:

> Suppose a Christian has savings to invest, and the choice is a building society or shares in a company making luxury cars. Then he will be right to choose the former, even if the prospect for monetary reward is much lower, on the grounds that it makes a greater contribution to society to help someone buy a house, than to provide for the production of expensive motor cars.[2]

If a property company wants to develop an area of old housing as a supermarket and business complex, Christians would do well to start or support protest groups who want to improve the houses and preserve homes.

In India similar decisions about land faced two Christian bodies. A church diocesan office had squatters on its land. These were the labourers who had built the church office. Some diocesan officials wanted to let the land to a lorry firm and allow the lorries to bulldoze them off. But more compassionate counsellors prevailed. They argued that the right of the squatters to somewhere to live, even if it was on church land, had priority over the church's rights to rent it at a large profit for missionary funds. In the second instance a Christian college wanted to construct new buildings. Some board members proposed that the college should surround the whole site with a large wall to keep the local village people out. But others asked why the college should come into an area and deprive villagers of the rights of way and grazing land for their animals. Early in his political life, 'God's Englishman', Oliver Cromwell, opposed measures by which landed gentry enclosed areas of common grazing land in order to develop it. Isaiah mapped out the principle: 'You are doomed! You buy more houses and fields to add to those you already have. Soon there will be nowhere for anyone else to live, and you alone will live in the land' (Isa. 5:8).

The second principle is that God takes the side of the poorest. The biblical commands to defend the widow and orphan are commands to side with those who are vulnerable, who will be last in the rat-race. So of any situation the Christian community must ask 'How will this legislation in operation affect the poorest?' and 'How can we effectively take their side?' This does not imply that the poorest are perfect and always right. It does mean that their case has claims on our attention. A Christian school in India began to discover what this meant. Near their gates three hundred people were living in an old single-story hotel with no water, sanitation, electric light – and even, in some rooms, no windows. The landlord decided that he wanted to develop the property. He accused his tenants of failing to pay rents, and refused to accept rent from them, so that he could legally evict them for non-payment of rent. Some of the school staff began to visit the slum and heard about this situation. They found that the only prospect for the tenants was that they would be evicted onto the streets. There was no alternative accommodation for them. So they encouraged the tenants to form a tenants' committee. This committee set up a rent collection agency which collected rent and deposited it in the bank to prove that rents were being paid. They also took up a court case against the landlord to prevent him evicting them. Gradually the tenants came to realise that they could work together to prevent themselves being exploited and ill-treated. They also took greater pride in their surroundings. They began to clean up the old premises and improve the sanitation. In the long term the Christian school is hoping to start a Building Society to construct low cost houses for low interest loans. But the process has not been easy. One of the school staff said 'The slum-dwellers lie to us, they deceive us and often we get very frustrated. Only commitment to Jesus and the fact that he is on the side of the poor people keeps us going'.

The third principle is that while God is on the side of the poor his challenge to the rich is that they should not seek security in their wealth. Jesus warned on many occasions that riches are dangerous. First they can keep men out of God's kingdom. After the rich young ruler turned away, Jesus commented that only God can do the impossible and help men renounce wealth to enter the kingdom (Mark 10:27). In the parable of the sower, he taught that love for riches was a major obstacle to spiritual growth (Mark 4:19). In the parable of the wedding feast, men's fields, oxen and marriage arrangements lead them to refuse God's invitation (Luke 14:15–24). Mammon is a rival divinity to God – it is impossible to serve both (Matt. 6:24). Riches cause men to get their priorities wrong.

Secondly, riches blind people to the needs of the poor. No one criticises the uncaring rich more fiercely than Jesus. He said they would go hungry, mourn and cry when God had his way (Luke 6:24). He mocked a successful businessman for planning expansion while failing to care for the poor. He called him a fool (Luke 12:13–20).

Jesus followed the parable of the rich fool with the familiar teaching of the Sermon on the Mount. Jesus makes the following points in Luke 12:22–34. He has warned the disciples in the parable of the rich fool: riches blind men to God's kingdom, for rich men tend to seek their security in wealth. Jesus enables men to renounce the pursuit of security in wealth. He encourages them to seek it in membership of God's kingdom. In God's kingdom God will provide the basic necessities of life for his subjects. So they have no need to use up energy and attention worrying about their own food, drink, clothing, length of life, the future, persecution or death. Instead, free of self-concern, they can give time and attention to his kingdom's standards of just relationships. Since God will provide their necessities, members of the kingdom can give to the poor. Giving money to the poor is saving treasures in heaven (Luke 12:33); and it enables trust in God to be expressed through giving to the poor. You give to the poor and find security in trusting that God will provide enough for your needs. Saving riches on earth expresses no trust in God, because you lay up riches for yourself. You do not give money, time or attention to the needs of the poor, because you need everything for your sense of security which is never satisfied.

So Jesus has a liberation for the rich! He sets them free from rebelling against God by seeking security in wealth. He sets them free to devote their attention and wealth to the concerns of God's kingdom, God's right relationships and especially the poor.

This third principle is probably the most relevant for English evangelicals. The gospel of Jesus Christ is not a vacuum-packed sterilised package delivered in identical packets to everyone's door. It is addressed personally to each one. The way the gospel addresses the rich is substantially different from the way it addresses the poor. Most English evangelicals are among the richest half of English and world society in terms of education, jobs, housing, access to power and income.

9: Poverty, injustice and development

In order to fully appreciate the meaning of the biblical material on God and the poor, we must study the world situation and map out some form of active response to the biblical material. We do not first discover biblical principles in their completeness from the Bible, and then go round to apply them. We actually discover their meaning as we seek to obey the injunctions in the Scripture in practice. Discipleship training must therefore include both biblically guided action, and reflection on the biblical material and on the results of our action. What then have evangelical Christians been learning from their work with poor people for development?

The Goal of Development

From its thirty years of experience, World Vision International now defines development in its policy documents as 'to move whole communities towards Christ'. A group of theologians and development practitioners in Madras expanded this statement in the following way:

> The goal of development is to help people and their communities be all that God intends them to be. This is possible only when people and communities acknowledge, experience and express the lordship of Christ in all aspects of their life.
>
> The task of development is to move people towards such a goal. This will involve making the proclamation of Christ a part of all development activity. This will also involve promoting Christian values in all development activities. The acceptance of these values moves people towards Christ.
>
> We will measure a community's progress towards acknow-

ledging the Lordship of Christ both by the individual's acceptance of Christ's Lordship, and by the community's response to and acceptance of Christian values, like servanthood towards all men, repentance of sin personal and corporate, and so on. These values are Christian in that they are patterned, empowered and complete in Christ, and express his Lordship.

This passage may be illustrated by the following diagram of Christian values.

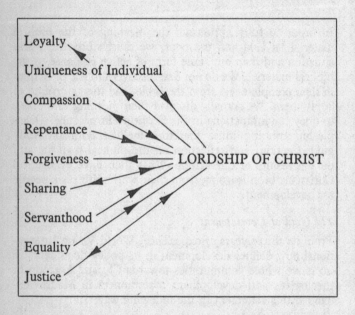

Loyalty

Uniqueness of Individual

Compassion

Repentance

Forgiveness — LORDSHIP OF CHRIST

Sharing

Servanthood

Equality

Justice

As we work for these Christian values through development, we are actually proclaiming that Jesus is Lord. We are moving a community towards accepting him as Lord because these values are finally based in his Lordship. For a community to understand, experience and express these values fully, they will need to acknowledge Jesus as Lord.

But not all communities who acknowledge Jesus as Lord express these values. Christian churches are often very little concerned for poor people. Sometimes they are riddled with self-interest and party strife. So we must also proclaim the reality of Jesus' Lordship in calling the Church to real discipleship and to incarnate the love of Christ in working for those values in a community. That is why the diagram has arrows pointing *both* ways.

This definition of the goal of development refers to moving whole communities towards Christ. Christians have often focused only on individuals. But as the Consultation on World Evangelisation in Thailand in June 1980 highlighted, we must also think of people as members of 'people-groups' and try and meet their needs as they perceive them. Probably the largest 'people-group' in the world is the poor. Waldron Scott, as general secretary of the World Evangelical Fellowship, pointed out at the Thailand Consultation that the unreached people of the world were by and large also the poor people of the world. Communists have had great success in tackling the problems and issues of a whole community, rather than isolating a few individuals from their community. Of course, each person must make a realistic personal submission to Jesus as Lord, but he may come to make that as a member of his group, once he has seen how Jesus challenges and brings good news to his group.

The task of 'moving whole communities towards Christ' is an evangelistic task. And the process of development in promoting values of justice and peace which express the lordship of Jesus is an essential part of that task. It is part of the whole mission of the church to men in their need. One understanding of the mission of the church which affirms this is the Madras Declaration of Evangelical Social Action (October 1979), which is reproduced as an appendix to this book.

Where Communities are

To engage in the process of moving people towards Christ we must have standards to assess where communities are, what their context is, what their needs are: in short, where they need to move *from* in their journey towards Christ.

We must examine a community's values. Values are re-

93

flected in the organisation of a community, how resources are produced and distributed, how the educational system is organised, how health, sanitation and welfare services are arranged, the patterns of employment and basis for pay, how decisions are made affecting the whole community and so on. Indian values are religiously sanctioned. Wealth is seen as a gift of God, a sign of his favour, however it has been obtained. The poverty of the poor is seen as God's punishment on them for wrongs committed in past lives. So Indian religion is by and large oppressive. It condemns over 60 per cent of India's population to accepting poverty, injustice and exploitation as their God-appointed fate.

We must examine the nature and causes of poverty in a community. The 'Evangelical Commitment to Simple Lifestyle' drawn up in March 1980, states 'Involuntary poverty . . . is related in the Bible to powerlessness, for the poor cannot protect themselves.' Without literacy, without access to any power, without knowledge of their rights in law, over 400 million people in India have no real choices in life. They live, work, suffer, and die where they are born. If they protest in any way they are sacked, silenced, or even have their mud huts burnt over their heads. They are easy prey to unscrupulous people who would exploit them. If the monsoon fails and food is short, poor villagers have to take out loans at between 50 and 75 per cent interest. Their lands or their children are security. When they fail to pay, the moneylenders seize their fields and their children to work for them. In the Bible such merciless exploitation and injustice is offensive to the goodness of God. It is not an expression of his will, as some other religions affirm.

Where communities should be

The Bible gives standards to assess where communities should be – what it will mean for a community to move towards Christ. The Bible gives a kaleidoscopic vision of just such a society of harmonious relationships. In the Mosaic law, provision was made to prevent pauperisation. The king was entrusted with protecting the poor from exploitation. The prophets looked forward to a new king who would rule the people with justice and defend the rights of the helpless (Isa. 11:4). The communities of the New Covenant were called to renounce discrimination between male and female, Jew and Greek, slave and free, adult and child, rich and poor.

Paul's description of the Body of Christ is of a society where each person has an indispensable contribution to make to the whole, where all must participate if the body is to function. Leadership is by service, and everyone can serve. In such a body, decision-making lies with the whole group. All must be enabled to love their neighbour, be servants, make their contributions and take part in leadership and decision-making. Power and leadership in the community are vested of course in the Head, Christ, who taught that his power was exercised as people served one another. So power and leadership belonged to all who would serve.

Christ is the new Adam, the true head of a new body of men and women who show what human relationships should be. The vision of the Body of Christ is not only for the church. It is for the world. This vision is the basis for claims that people should be in control of their own lives, and not manipulated or exploited by others; that they should have a part in decisions that affect them, that they should be able to make choices that benefit the whole community, that they should be able to develop their potentials to serve others; in short that the focus of power should be with people. John Staley, a former director of Oxfam in South India, sums up these claims as components of the development process: all people's basic needs will be met, there will be a greater economic, social and political equality and justice, people will gain greater control over their lives and less control over the lives of others, people will move from reliance and dependency on others to self-reliance and interdependence with others, power will be more evenly distributed throughout society, and people will co-operate with one another rather than compete against each other.[1] Many movements in history have had this vision of human society. Only the motivation and power of the Spirit of Christ's servanthood can prevent such movements becoming, in time, as exploitative as the systems they seek to replace, or foundering on the rocks of human selfishness. Power will truly lie with the people when all the people are servants.

How will we move communities towards Christ?

How will we be able to move communities from where they are to where they ought to be? The process is not obvious. Many Christians and Christian organisations assume that once the obligation to love our poor neighbour is accepted, the process of *how* to love him will be obvious. The very existence of intense global discussion on this issue shows that what may be obvious to some is not obvious to others. There are many Christians now engaged in a number of processes for moving people towards Christ which are at least questionable in their biblical basis, and in their results.

Some Christians argue that if we verbally proclaim the gospel, enable people to change their religious commitment and increase the number of churches, then a change in values and in social injustice will be automatic. If we concentrate on verbal proclamation of the gospel, social change will look after itself.

First, this approach may not be biblical. Jesus did not make quantitative growth in the numbers of his disciples the means whereby the good news would act as leaven in society. Instead in the Sermon on the Mount he focused on the quality of discipleship as the leaven, the salt and the light which the world needed. Secondly, it is doubtful whether Jesus made a separate process of a spiritual commitment to him as Lord which would later produce the fruits of discipleship. He called men to follow him directly in costly discipleship which involved stances against social injustice. He said that he was 'The Way, the Truth and the Life'. Vinay Samuel writes:

> This was not an offer to give people 'life' as they stood still, apart from the world, and held out their hands to receive. It was as people followed in the way, in the costly way of the

96

cross, in taking a stance by renouncing riches, repaying frauds, or forgiving seventy times seven, that they would experience the life that was this stance and that would sustain this stance.[2]

Thirdly, it is not certain how far this approach moves communities towards experiencing and expressing the Lordship of Christ. There are many countries which have a sizeable Christian population who are not distinguished by their social justice or compassion. In India some pragmatic Christians argue that churches grow more quickly if new believers are not asked to cross caste-lines in joining the church. In the West, many churches meet along such 'interest-lines', middle-class white suburban Christians meet totally separately all the time from working class or black Christian groups. But such a practice in India reinforces social oppression. The weight of religiously sanctioned caste-prejudice (or group self-interest) prevents a labourer's son ever becoming anything else except a labourer. If the church sanctions caste in the interests of growth, is it truly bringing good news of a new humanity in Christ, or is it leaving oppression unchallenged?

A second process which many Christians follow is to send money to give to Christian groups in the Third World who are trying to witness to Christ through proclamation or through relief and welfare schemes. We must ask whether the relationship thus set up between donors and recipients encourages true growth or dependency. Graham Houghton has researched the life of the church in Madras since 1860 and discovered that once a pattern of dependency between donor and recipient Christians was established, it impoverished the growth of the recipient groups and proved impossible to break. Dependency never matures into anything else.[3]

Rather we should follow the pattern of partnership found in Romans 14 and 15, where the strong do not dominate, manipulate or make the weak dependent. Instead they share their power. Vinay Samuel and Charles Corwin suggest guidelines for true partnership in *Assistance Programs Require Partnership*.[4] They contend that mere affluence should not qualify a group to assume the donor role. Churches should decide together who will be donor and who recipient for a particular project. If a Third World church is designated the receptor church for a particular programme, then there must be real partnership in decision-making and implementation; just as, if a First World church were designated as the receptor church for a teaching ministry by a Third World team, that church would expect to be closely involved in the decision-making and implementation. National leaders must take a full part in decision-making; they are best qualified to specify the real needs. It may be better for fund-raising and publicity to provide ten villages with drinking water: but it may actually be better for the villagers if they could regain the land which they have lost through the system of debt-slavery.

There must also be partnership in implementing assistance programmes. Often the representatives of the donor-culture select the leaders who affirm their values and ways of doing things. Such people become dependent on western agencies and have no need to develop responsibility to the churches in their own society. This is the multi-national corporation model of world partnership; not the Christian model.

True partnership frees the donor from concealing his own needs, weaknesses and inexperience and from pretending to expertise which he does not have. He can learn and receive gifts and direction from the receptor-culture while serving it. The receptor will be freed from feelings of inferiority and be given boldness to share his gifts. The church must show how the weak can develop to safety and confidence in a mature relationship with the strong. Christians cannot call for a new just international economic order if they are not prepared to share power with, and receive from, national Christians in the Third World.

A third process which Christians favour is to save money through a simple lifestyle in the west to send money to set up specific projects which aim at the economic benefit for a community while avoiding any issues that might be construed as political. These projects will demonstrate the love of Christians and, by including proclamation of the gospel, will hope to share the good news of Christ.

This process is not necessarily biblical. First it makes the mistake of measuring poverty solely in economic terms. Cut down expenditure in one place, increase it in another and poverty will be removed. Jesus did not see life like that. He saw it in terms of good and evil, obedience to God, disobedience, righteousness and wickedness, covetousness and sharing, trusting in God and trusting in Mammon, judgement, repentance, forgiveness and reconciliation. If the problem in a society is social injustice and oppression – wrong human relationships rooted in rebellion against God – and if the gospel is about right human relationships rooted in love of God, then by addressing wrong human relationships (which are the issues of social and political life) with the judgement and grace of the gospel, both on the personal and corporate level, we are announcing the good news of the kingdom.

If we merely import economic betterment we demonstrate that we are ignorant of what secular agencies have found out, that economic betterment only betters the better off. Epstein writes of development in the last fifteen years in our state of Karnataka in South India:

A process of increasing economic differentiation . . . has taken place . . . The wealthiest farmers have become considerably richer. The jaggery boom provided the possibility of a windfall profit to all farmers who owned more than two or three wet acres: the greater the cane acreage the greater the benefit the farmer derived from the soaring jaggery prices. This encouraged the wealthier and more enterprising peasants to invest in more and more wet land, as well as in cane crushers to process their crop into jaggery. . . . [there was] a cumulative process of concentration of wealth in the hands of a small elite of peasant farmers.[5]

Besides failing to learn from the observations and failures of others, we will also reduce the scope of our Christian witness to showing that we can love and serve, instead of also enabling others to love and serve in turn.

Secondly, many processes of economic betterment have

an implicit view of man which is not necessarily biblical. The following story from Colombia illustrates this: a highly respected national leader of the Colombian church was reviewing an animal loan project with his North American evangelical colleague. The project was designed to help church families improve their diet and build economic independence. 'Starter' animals were given to a few families; gradually the stewardship/ownership plan was extended to additional families as new animals were born. Yet the Colombian was uneasy. 'We can't do it this way', he finally announced.

'Why not?' asked the startled missionary.

'Because they're making a profit.'

But that's what we want, don't we?'

'No, we are brothers, not capitalists.'[6]

10: Communities on the move

How shall we then proceed to move communities towards Christ? We are beginning to learn that Jesus was concerned with justice and justification, with social and personal righteousness before God. This concern has chiefly been expressed in social service. In India social service has been shown through schools and hospitals, to bind up the wounds of the completely destitute and provide help within the existing structures. But the social relationships of God's kingdom run counter to the relationships promoted by many social structures. For people who live in poverty and under oppression to become truly self-sufficient, to develop their own lives and have a sense of dignity and self-worth, it is not sufficient to provide them merely with health and education services. For them to live in just social relationships, enjoy a measure of equality and think of themselves as valuable human beings with rights that should not be denied them, it is necessary that exploitative and unjust social relationships should be recognised and addressed.

The history of the church in the world is full of examples of Christians confronting those who support and promote injustice: the Anabaptist movement (the Mennonites), Calvin's discussion of political disobedience, the American colonists, Wilberforce's campaign against the slave trade and Shaftesbury's campaign against exploitative employers. In India those examples are not repeated so often, because of the colonial past of the Indian Church. The independent Church in India has unthinkingly taken this political conditioning. As one leading Trades Unionist in Bangalore put it, the first article of faith for Christians in India is often 'Thou shalt support the party in power'. This position is

101

reinforced by theological arguments, but it is not necessarily biblical.

Jesus, as we see in our study of his ministry, firmly based the search for justice in human society on the justice of God. He upheld the dignity of human life on the basis of a new self-image of people; creatures of God, who can become sons of God. Acceptance of his teaching and his Lordship can lead to a process of judgement, repentance and reconciliation which does not merely replace one group of oppressors with another.

One example of unjust social structures in India is the way many grants, loans and resources which are earmarked for the poor through banks and other organisations are not available to them. A process of Christian development without foreign funds is seeking justice by encouraging poor people to make representations so that they receive this help, which is their right. Another example is the way unorganised labour in small scale industries in cities is mercilessly exploited. Employers honour labour laws more in the breach than in the practice. Again, Christians have begun to seek justice and development by planning for legal advice and legal aid for these workers. In the villages, many villagers are held in bondage to their landowners throughout their lives. They have never made a decision independently of him. A process which would encourage the villagers to decide independently of their landlord to improve their lot would give them confidence in their ability to make their own decisions, and would open the way for them eventually to make a decision for Christ.

Many situations in poor countries require that Christians take clear sides against exploitation. But it is not easy for evangelical relief and development agencies to support Christians who seek to take sides with the exploited. There is great pressure on fund-raising groups, as on political parties, to take middle-of-the road positions in order to attract the widest possible support. Not everyone who gives to a development agency would approve of Christians taking sides in this way. So, despite their claims that they take the whole gospel to the whole man, evangelical relief and development agencies are often prevented from carrying out the full implications of this and from taking clear sides on an issue of justice for fear of losing financial support.

It is vital that those who support the radical demands of the gospel should encourage evangelical agencies to carry out their claim to bring the whole gospel to the whole man. If they do not meet an adequate response, they should perhaps seek alternative ways of promoting wholistic mission in the Two-Thirds World.

The Church in the West can give moral support and fellowship to Third World Christians as they seek to move their communities towards the Lordship of Christ, the Prince of right relationships, in such ways. They might also learn from the process to look at similar problems in their own society and how they can tackle them.

Certainly all Christians need to examine the values and the vision they have for a just society and how to get there by biblical criteria. I do not claim to have spelt out those criteria in detail. In many ways the process of discovering them is just beginning. But the process will be carried on as the community of God's Spirit – the Spirit of Jesus – is open to the Word of the Spirit in the Scriptures, as it seeks the fellowship of the Spirit with Christians throughout the world in different situations, and as they seek the meaning of the Scriptures through action carried out in obedience to them.

How do people develop?

How can this situation of powerlessness and poverty be changed? One method which is now being seriously attempted is as follows. In ones and twos people make contact with villagers and slum dwellers. They find out a few who are dissatisfied with the present situation. They meet with them to learn the particular problems in the area, and to help them to understand some of the reasons for the problems – and the rights that are guaranteed to them by the constitution of the country. The discussion group tries to find some action which will amend the problem under discussion and attempts to do it.

For example: a church in Bombay wanted to help a group of slum dwellers. They discovered that there was no water connection in the slum. The church did not apply to Christian relief organisations to bore a tube well because that would be doing things for the people and not with them. The lack of water was because the corporation of Bombay had not fulfilled its responsibility in this and other ways to provide basic human needs. If they provided a bore well that would have been a superficial solution to a deep-seated problem. The people needed to gain the confidence and self respect of uniting together to firmly request the corporation to do its duty and provide a water connection. But the local landowner did not want the pipes for their water connection to cross his land. He did his best to thwart the slum dwellers' application. It took two years to get the water connection – but the slum dwellers got more than their water. They learnt how to act together to withstand the apathy of bureaucracy, the power of money and their own innate passivity in the face of injustice.

In Nagpur in central India a group of Christians made contacts with the men who pulled cycle rickshaws – a three wheeled cycle with a seat for two at the back. 6000 men hired their rickshaws from fifty owners for 30 pence a day. Their total day's takings would be 60 pence. Over the years some had paid enough in hiring charges to buy twenty rickshaws; but they were still hiring them each day. This group of Christians discussed the men's problems with them. Various solutions were tried – loans to buy their own rickshaws failed, because none of the owners would sell. The Christians were able to provide a hall where the rickshaw pullers could repair the vehicles, which was (unfairly) their responsibility. They also discussed with the men the cause of their problems. Eventually the men decided to ask the local MP to request the State government to transfer the ownership of all rickshaws to the pullers without compensation. And the State government did so. So the rickshaw pullers' earnings doubled overnight.

This programme of development to enable people to make their own choices about caring for their family, and about working together to achieve just treatment, involves Christians who have education and skills identifying themselves with poor people. They must learn to see problems from their perspective rather than condemn them as lazy or drunk. They must show that they want to work *with* the people so that the people can improve themselves, rather than that they are working from above for 'unfortunate' people down below. In short, they must communicate respect for them. They must also be prepared to lose the respect of other peer groups. When floods filled some huts with silt, a Christian lay preacher donned his gum boots and worked with the people clearing the mess. A member of his congregation saw him and told her friends she would never listen to another sermon from a man who worked in wellington boots! Identification is part of incarnation, of which crucifixion is the result.

Working with people also involves understanding them; and that takes time. In India, it means people sit and listen to poor people talking about their problems. Even this action gives respect and dignity which is normally denied them. One slum community felt Christians in a nearby church despised them. So two girls from the church who were school teachers went visiting and listening. They began extra classes for the children in the evenings. Now six people in the slum work as teachers in their evening school for ninety children.

In the West, it means taking time to understand the real causes of poverty and powerlessness. This hurts because it questions many assumptions we have about life. To get us started there are magazines like 'New Internationalist' and books like *How the Other Half Dies* by Susan George (Penguin). Our study may focus on a country in which we have an interest, or a consumer product we buy which is the product of exploited labour in the Third World. But such study may be the first real education we receive on how things really are in the world.

Western Christians can play a part in changing the situ-

105

ation in the Third World in a number of ways. *They can pray*. So ingrained is the system of injustice in our world, so deep-seated is evil and man's rebellion that prayer, the spiritual weapon of God's kingdom, is essential. *They can encourage* Christians in Third World countries who are struggling against injustice. *They can find out* what they are doing, learn from them and show their interest and concern. *They can help* the task of changing the values in a Third World culture by supporting the national church's witness to the total dimension of God's kingdom with personnel and finance.

Visits by Western Christians to learn what is really going on have a real place. There will always be a role for Western Christians to live alongside national churches to share their struggles and communicate what national churches are discovering about Christian obedience in their culture. Traffic will be two-way. Christians in the West are learning from Christian struggles for justice in South Africa, Latin America and India that they must be involved in issues of justice in Europe and America.

Two lecturers from an American evangelical seminary were visiting development projects in India. They discovered that before they could teach their American students any more about development, they would have to involve them in the lives and problems of a black ghetto a few miles away. And until Christians in the West become involved in deprived areas and problems of justice in the West, the process of exporting their concern to Africa or India will be hollow. For the message Indian Christians receive is this. 'Western Christians live in a wealthy society. They have excess money which they send to us to do something about poverty here. The only way to do something about poverty here is to be identifying with the problems and struggles of poor people. But we do not see the Christians in the West involved in those difficult problems over there. So clearly Christians don't need to be involved in the real pains of development. They can become rich, avoid the real issues and send money to help the poor. So we will try to escape these problems ourselves and pass on the West's money to the poor.'

Western Christians should model a form of Christian life-style which is personally identified with or involved in issues of justice. Chris Wigglesworth writes: 'The Indian Church will take more heart from seeing the Church in Britain sweating and being laughed at. It will give the Church in India heart to be exposed itself . . . we need to feel we are bound together in the fellowship of Christ's sufferings.'[1]

The critical issue of lifestyle is not that simple living by itself saves money to send to the poor. Both my wife and I returned separately for short vists to England after eighteen months in India. We both felt far less concerned about England's affluence than when we left. We had learnt that cash itself is not the issue. We used to think that is was. But we began to see that to focus on less expenditure in England so that money could be sent to India was to accept a materialistic analysis of the world. Jesus did not make such an analysis. He put the focus on God, other people and right relationships.

We are now coming to see that the issue is whether Christians in showing God's concern for the whole person are committed to work for justice and God's right relationships in their area, especially for the powerless and deprived. This may involve sharing scarce resources, developing old housing, living in the inner city, trading in Third World goods, running a playgroup for working mums, working for a trades union, campaigning against unfair Tariff barriers on Third World goods, pressing for jobs to be created for unemployed people, working part-time in a hospital or old-people's home, or teaching immigrant housewives English. If we are concerned with these things, with God's kingdom and its right relationships, we will find that they so dominate our time, attention and resources that we can manage very well on the necessities that God provides and don't need to attend to luxuries.

How can the resources of the West be shared? One way that we feel very positive about is sharing in the training of people. It has been our privilege to share in the training of young Indian men and women, not in the West or in Indian universities, but through exposing them to the actual realities of deprivation and injustice, and reflecting with them from the Bible on how to work for God's standards of social justice. The Educational and Training Unit of the Evangelical Fellowship of India Commission of Relief has been located on our church premises, and over two years has trained 40 young people to live and work alongside villagers and slum dwellers to work with them for change. Other young people from England and America have come to be exposed to the reality of the Indian situation and to see how the Indian church is seeking to bring the whole gospel to the whole man, so that they can be true partners in this process when they return to the West. These training and exposure programmes are a very valuable way of sharing resources and partnering the Indian church in its mission.

11: Teaching by evangelism

My goal, then, is to present each person mature in Christ, able to express and enjoy God. We are seeking to encourage people to grow gradually into a stable relationship with God, to be able to apply biblical truths to their daily living and to have an intellectual grip on the Gospel – appropriate to their intelligence. We must enable them to understand the issues of the world so that they are better equipped to act as salt in a decaying society. We must help them to understand themselves, to recognise their own gifts and provide them with opportunities to express these gifts as members of the Body of Christ.[1]

To achieve this goal we will not present people with a set of the 'latest' answers. We have no examples of Jesus handing out an all-embracing set of doctrines to people. He started with people's own questions and life situation. He then led them to see how God's word and will was relevant to their own situation.

We will best teach radical discipleship by helping people to interact the Scriptures with their personal and social questions and problems. The expression of the good news of the arrival of God's kingdom in Jesus will differ in each social context. In the loneliness of Western industrial society, Jesus' friendship and the fellowship of the Christian community addresses the good news to people's real needs. In India loneliness is not such a pressing problem. But millions suffer intolerable injustices from which they see no escape and which religious teaching has schooled them to accept as fate. Injustice and oppression is often seen as the gods' punishment on poor and low-caste people. The religious and cultural system then absorbs or even rejects all attempts at protest or reform. The good news in this situation is that the one God judges injustice and creates new just relationships based on forgiveness and reconciliation. In Christ all barriers are broken down and there is a new creation.

New Christians will learn to interact Scripture with a life situation, rather than reproduce a pre-packaged message through the methods of evangelism they are exposed to. We cannot hold evangelistic practices to be above criticism on the grounds that God has blessed them. Someone may become a Christian as the result of a failed suicide attempt; but we would not therefore advocate attempted suicide as an evangelistic method! God's blessing is always a result of his mercy. But his blessing cannot excuse us from critical evaluation of our methods in the light of Scripture, unless we want to believe that his blessing is because of our good works.

Evangelism

Evangelism is making known the evangel, the good news of the kingdom of God as announced and inaugurated by Jesus Christ. The kingdom of God is God's kingdom of right relationships, of righteousness, between God and man, and man and man and his environment. The kingdom was inaugurated by Jesus Christ, and will be consummated at his return. The call of Jesus to men and women to follow him was a call to obey him, to enjoy the right relationships of the kingdom, and take the stance of the kingdom in the society of the day. The kingdom is here, so enter it and enjoy it, and express it.

The goal of evangelism is that people should enter the kingdom, or to put it another way, should acknowledge that Jesus Christ is Lord, Lord of history, Lord of their land and Lord of their lives. This acknowledgement is not to be by word only, but is to be expressed in action. The goal of evangelisation is that people acknowledge and express the Lordship of Christ. In the scriptures this acknowledgement cannot be divorced from membership of a community which expresses the Lordship of God in its relationships, in its fellowship, its sharing, its concern for righteousness, its bias for the poor.

The Theological Work Group of the Nationwide Initiative in Evangelism (which included both Roman Catholics and Evangelicals) produced the following statement on evangelism in June 1980:

> 'Evangelism is like one beggar telling another where to find bread' (D. T. Niles). Christ still sends all his followers into the world as his witnesses. Christians commend not themselves but the love of God as known in Jesus. What we are and do is no less important than what we say. As we humbly but joyfully reflect God's reconciling love for all humanity, in friendship and respect, the Holy Spirit uses our witness and service to make God known. The joy of sharing good news simply because it is good is the common joy of all Christians. God has exalted Jesus to his right hand, that every knee should bow to him and every tongue confess that he is Lord (Phil. 2:9–11).[2]

How should we evangelise?

How should we make the good news known? In the Scriptures the model we are presented with as the climax of God's communication of the good news to men is the incarnation of Jesus. The incarnation has several important features:

Communication through incarnation is specific to a context. Jesus came as a Jew to Jews. He did not come as a universal man. Therefore incarnation has a context in which it is involved. It is not general and universal. Jesus did not just speak to Jews, he became a Jew. He identified himself with all aspects of being a Jew.

Incarnation takes the cultural context seriously. Jesus came into the real problems, debates, issues and struggles of the Jewish people, and within those struggles and debates he took a distinct and significant stance. Incarnation means involvement in the economic, social and political relationships of society, with distinctive attitudes.

Incarnation takes humanity seriously. Jesus became truly one man in a context, not any man in any context.

Incarnation takes the audience seriously. He did not address

111

the Jews as though they were symbolic figures representing all men before God. He did not address them impersonally, separate from their contexts. He came to his own, and spelt out his claims in terms that spoke uniquely to Jews. He claimed to be fulfilling the mission of the Jewish Messiah.

Jesus, then, while on earth did not communicate the good news of the kingdom through a universal message, abstracted from any cultural specifics, equally applicable impersonally to all men in all times and in all places. He did not speak a 'universal language'. His evangelism could not be reduced to a message, for it also consisted in his incarnation, his stances, his involvement. His whole person, his being a Jew, his actions and attitudes were set in the Jewish context. They have universal implications it is true, but they are not stated or presented in universal terms. Incarnation is contextual, and so is meaningful, challenging and inescapable. You can't run away from incarnation.

The incarnation gives us a number of guidelines for our evangelism.

First, *we communicate by incarnating the message*. Jesus said 'I am the truth', not 'I give you the truth'. The best way to communicate Jesus is to incarnate his lifestyle.

Secondly, *we are to communicate to people in their context*. A major question we must examine in any evangelisation is: who are we evangelising, and what is their context? Incarnational evangelism addresses people in their economic, social, political and personal relationships in their actual context. We must communicate with people as they are, as they perceive themselves to be. Increasingly, it is being realised that Jesus spoke with various groups in Jewish society. He did not always address people as isolated individuals. And sociologically it is being recognised that people perceive themselves as members of groups with their own set of needs and problems. So the concept is arising of addressing people as 'people's groups', and making a careful study of how they perceive themselves and what they perceive their needs to be. These people groups cover people in their social, economic, political and religious existence. We must examine that context carefully, not only sociologically, but theologically. What is there in people's contexts which is preventing them responding to the good news of Jesus? Are they a group which is blinded to the good news because of a preoccupation with wealth? Are they a group which is as much the object of sin and oppression by other people and social structures as they are the subject of sin? How will the gospel be perceived as good news by these people? In the New Testament we see that Jesus addressed his good news to the rich and the oppressing groups in terms of judgemental calls for repentance. We find less stress on this when he is addressing groups of poor and socially outcast people.

Third, since we are to address an incarnated message to people in their cultural contexts, *we must seriously ask 'What is the gospel in this context?'* For the New Testament the gospel is Jesus Christ, its content is Jesus Christ. The person and work of Jesus Christ according to the scripture is the gospel (1 Cor. 15:1–15). But when we ask the question 'What themes of the gospel are especially relevant to this group whom the writer is addressing?', we find within the unity of the scriptural proclamation a rich diversity of expressions and formulations relevant to different groups. John emphasises that Jesus is God become man. Paul emphasises that God freely forgives us in Christ because of his death. James emphasises that people demonstrate their faith in Christ through good works. Luke stresses that the gospel is the power of God at work, especially on the side of the poor. All these were different emphases of the meeting of the gospel of Jesus Christ in different contexts. Our commitment to the authority of the Scriptures means that we accept that those formulations in those contexts are normative expressions of the incarnated gospel. The writer of Revelation correctly contextualised the gospel of Jesus Christ for those who trusted Jesus in situations of great persecution.

How then can we announce the gospel of Jesus Christ in our context in a way that is faithful to the scriptural proclamation?

First, *is the Jesus we present, the Jesus of the Gospels?* One

113

Saturday a senior choir girl in our church in Bangalore complained bitterly to the pastor that she had been handed her pay for singing at a wedding by the church gardener. The pastor asked her if the gardener was a dog who was not good enough to pass on a gift. The Jesus this girl had learnt about in twenty years of Sunday School and Christian schools was not the Jesus of Galilee who ate with all classes of men. He was a stained-glass Christ who made her a nice girl ready for heaven.

Secondly, *is our presentation honest?* It is not uncommon for some preachers to begin an evangelistic message (in word or print) with a catalogue of contemporary problems in politics, corruption, drugs, sex, poverty or war. So far so good. They then reduce all these problems to one issue, personal sin illustrated by lust, anger or selfishness; and from then on they talk only about personal forgiveness. Such preachers deceive their hearers into thinking that Christians are genuinely concerned about the larger issues when really they are giving the Christian community excuses for avoiding them. John the Baptist and Jesus called tax-collectors to repent specifically of their involvement in social injustice. They did not separate *kerygma*, the good news of the kingdom, from *didache*, the teaching about the life of the kingdom. Both repentance and didache are present in the gospels and both are largely absent from many evangelistic presentations.

Thirdly, *is our presentation relevant?* The world sets the agenda for the concerns of God's people. Jesus and the prophets spoke to the men and problems of their time in detailed terms. They did not utter airy generalisations. We must speak to the actual situations men are in and bring God's redemption to those situations. Therefore to some extent we must begin with the burning issues of our time and go back to the biblical resources to understand and respond to them. Dr. Carl Henry identifies abortion as a vital issue calling for Christian witness in America. For Jim Wallis, editor of *Sojourners* magazine and identified by *Time* magazine as one of fifty young American leaders to watch, the issue is the spread of nuclear power for peaceful uses as well as in war.

In Britain Roy Dorey identifies this issue:

> If urban and industrial life isolates people, and reduces their view of their own value, then it is at this point that the Christian faith has something clear to say.

Stemming from the New Testament demand for individual responsibility towards God is the sense that individuals

> are valuable in themselves and not just as a way of meeting the needs of other people . . . In presenting the gospel of God we are not stepping in where society stops by filling the gap of 'being needed' by others. We are showing the nature of God as someone who cares for his creation and his creatures, and the nature of humankind in that a relationship with the living God is the destined purpose for which it was created. We shall incidentally but importantly be making comments on sin and failure, but in view of the kind of society that we all live in, the nature of the gospel must be made clear in wider terms than meeting the individual need of salvation at a particular time of repentance.[3]

In Britain no less than in India the gospel gives worth, value and confidence to the council estate tenant, the machine operative, the landless labourer or slum dweller.

Fourthly, *is our presentation complete*? Do we visualise the gospel, as well as verbalise it? Do we combine ministries of teaching and healing with the same balance that Jesus did? In Bombay one church communicates Jesus Christ by running a club for the children who live on the city's pavements. The club shares God's love and hope with these children and demonstrates, to the middle class members of the church, God's prejudice for the poor.

Does our presentation show that the God revealed in Jesus Christ is a God of justice as well as justification? Dr. Carl Henry says:

> If we only consider justification, the forgiven sinner has a limited concept of the sin from which God justifies him. If we neglect the God of justice in our preaching we shrink the idea of what God saves us from. Therefore we must show that

structures which are meant to promote justice and which are now instruments of injustice are intolerable and unacceptable to the God of justice. Christians have a calling to criticise them. Some Christians may have a special vocational call to evangelism but no one is called to neglect justice. Evangelism remains an indispensable aspect of the church's social thrust for justice. For any change in structures or society must be sustained by the good will of people. The attitudes and motivations of those who want to protect the status quo are crucial. The key to changing these is the matter of an altered mind and heart.[4]

Finally, *does our unprogrammed evangelism present Jesus Christ faithfully?* How we handle the emotions of love, anger, guilt, forgiveness, joy and peace in ourselves and in others, shows the sort of God we really believe in. If our church preaches a gospel of free grace, and yet the elders leave the young people to specialists, exclude unmarried mothers, and hope the immigrants will join a church in their own coloured community, they show they do not understand what justification by grace through faith means. Like the Galatian Christians, they are making acceptance by the congregation – and so, by God – depend on status and human merit.

Our evangelism should be growing out of the life of the church. As Morgan Derham writes:

> Growth is the outworking of life. Evangelism is the overflow of a living growing experience of God. When rain falls in the hills, the springs flow in the valleys![5]

Evangelism should be springing from a church life that proclaims that Jesus is Lord of all life through the involvement of Christian groups and individuals. Does a congregation show that Jesus' attitudes determine their decisions on what they spend their money on, how they are involved in the life of the local community, what they do about social problems? As new Christians are drawn into the life of such a church, they are already set on the right course. The involvement of a church in visiting a battered wives home, in working with a local Shelter housing group, and building bridges with immigrant communities in England will set the style of what discipleship is all about. In a city-wide evangelistic campaign in Leeds, black and white churches came together for united festivals of praise. When the campaign ended, black Christians naturally expected to be welcomed more regularly to the worship and fellowship of white churches, and it is to be hoped that out of such beginnings the churches will model a genuinely multicultural society where barriers of colour are a thing of the past. In South India visiting Mother Teresa's orphanage and teaching slum children has set a style of discipleship for some young people.

New Christians joining the church will expect to demonstrate through the Christian community what they have seen and heard. They will provide a continual blood transfusion for local churches. In the U.S.A. Chuck Colson has not remained as a trophy of grace for evangelicals to gloat over. God has used him to awaken the evangelical church to issues of prison reform to such an extent, according to Carl Henry, that it has now become an important part of evangelical social concern.

12: Teaching by calling to repentance

> If Jesus Christ is Lord, men must be confronted with his authority over the totality of life. Evangelism is not a mere offer of benefits achieved by Jesus Christ: Christ's work is inseparable from his person; the Jesus who died for our sins is the Lord of the whole universe, the announcement of forgiveness in his name is inseparable from the call to repentance, the call to turn from the rulers of this world to the Lord of glory.[1]

The good news is that God's kingdom of justice and right relationships has burst into history in the person of the risen Lord. Men cannot continue to live as if nothing had happened. They must repent before they can enter the kingdom.

Repentance will mean redirecting their lives by adopting a lifestyle that is attuned to the new age that has invaded this old age. Repentance is not simply abandoning bad habits condemned by a personal moral code. Men must accept the cross of Christ as their death to natural, cultural or acceptable standards for evaluating human life: they must no longer identify success in terms of advancement, status, recognition, or income: they must no longer reckon achievement in terms of economic growth or education: they can no longer trust in throwing dollars at problems or manipulating the system. The kingdom announces that these are false standards, and experience confirms this. The success criterion has created a ruthless law of the jungle in the western world: the Eldorado of economic growth cripples human rights and dignity in many developing countries: dollars thrown at problems mostly end in the wrong pockets. In the kingdom God's justice is established especially for the poor, social barriers are crossed, achievement is measured in terms of service, and victory often comes only through defeat.

Repentance is not a question of feelings of sorrow, guilt or bad conscience, sadness which is merely human and causes death (2 Cor. 7:10). A repentant person accepts the judgement of God on human values and achievements. He identifies with Jesus as Jesus represented him on the cross, taking the consequences of rebellion. He trusts in the new life promised. He submits to Jesus' Lordship by seeking to express the life of the new age in behaviour empowered by the Holy Spirit.

A Sikh was recently converted in North India. He owned a haulage firm. Before his conversion, to keep his business growing, he engaged in activities of which the Mafia would have been proud. When he became a Christian he repented – or rather he felt guilty and sorry because of problems in his family. He did nothing to repent or make amends for murder, looting and arson. No less problematical are Western businessmen who repent of illicit sex and never question the activities of the company they work for.

John the Baptist told men to prepare for the coming of the kingdom of heaven by repenting of their sins. He directed his call for repentance to peoples' home and business addresses. Ordinary people who in the midst of the daily round and common task were overwhelmed with the needs of their own family and job were told to share with the poor. He warned tax collectors to collect no more than their due, and not to use public office for private gain. He asked soldiers not to abuse their power by extorting loot from a subject population. Complacency, corruption and misuse of power were everyday realities and came under the spotlight when John announced the kingdom. But today much Christian moralising attacks sins that few people are guilty of and which most people condemn – euthanasia, drug taking and hard pornography.

John did not address people as sinners in the abstract or as individuals in isolation from their social role. He did not accuse tax-collectors of being bad fathers or drunken husbands (though they may have been that also). He saw them in their social role and called for them to repent. John was aware of issues of justice. Extortion was not only bad for the spiritual purity of the soldiers, it was very painful for their victims. Complacency was not an unfortunate weakness in people's lives, it condemned others to nakedness. In fact, his call to people with two coats to share one of them with someone who had none sounds more like a call to sacrifice than to repent. But the Jewish law had provisions to prevent pauperisation. If there were poor people, it meant the law had been flouted. The whole community was responsible. So John's call was for repentance for complicity in social sin. The fruit was to be neither charity nor sacrifice, but a restoration to the poor of the rights which the law guaranteed to them.

Often Christians indulge in ethics divorced from the context of justice. They ask what behaviour will least compromise their purity rather than what behaviour will best promote justice. Start a discussion in a Bible study about joining trade unions and see what I mean.

Repentance also means repentance for corporate sin. When Isaiah confessed that he was a man of unclean lips and dwelt among a people of unclean lips he was associating himself with the sins of the Israelite people. The first five chapters of his prophecy show that these include religion without concern for justice, corrupt rulers, oppressive moneylenders, landlords who bought up the land of the poor, and laws which protected such exploitation (Isa. 10:1–2). Amos indicts luxuriant women who make excessive demands on their husbands and so force them to exploit the poor to meet their demands. Their social life and fine clothes are won by the sweat and tears of toiling peasants (Amos 4:1). Amos underlies the judgement of Ronald Sider: 'If one is a member of a privileged class that profits from institutional evil and does nothing to try and change things, one stands guilty before God.'[2]

Repentance is not complete when mind, attitudes and values are changed. It must bear fruit in behaviour. Zacchaeus demonstrated the reality of his repentance and validity of his salvation when he repaid the money he had cheated from people. It is not enough to declare one has no racial prejudice or no special attachment to material possessions. Some active detachment is needed. Finding forgiveness through the cross is not a static process of cancelling past guilt. Atonement is a static term not found in the New Testament. We are indeed forgiven for past sin but only in order to be reconciled with God and enter an ongoing service in submission to Jesus as Lord.

Reconciliation with God must include and lead to reconciliation with others, especially those of other social groups. Paul told masters to love their servants, not fellow-masters: husbands to love their wives, not their business partners. For Jesus, loving enemies and social outcasts typified the right relationships of God's kingdom. Jesus' way of establishing God's justice and right relationships was not just to forgive men of their past. He reached across social, cultural and religious barriers to create new relationships of justice. Jews of the period would have denounced and punished the hated Zacchaeus, Chief of Tax Collectors, who soiled his hands by daily contact with Gentiles, took his cut of the taxes he collected and collaborated with the hated Romans. Jesus asked to come to his house, touch his unclean hands and utensils, and sit at his table. Jesus reached out with forgiveness and reconciliation across the barriers and created justice. Zacchaeus responded by offering fourfold restitution to those he had cheated.

Biblical repentance is a message of hope. When people heard John denouncing the tax-collectors and soldiers we read 'People's hopes began to rise, and they began to wonder whether John might perhaps be the Messiah' (Luke 3:15). John's preaching assured them that God saw injustice and was calling those responsible to account.

John's preaching also assured people that beyond repentance lay the assurance of forgiveness. God's purpose of winnowing was not to dispose of the chaff so much as to gather in the grain of a people obedient to him. The Messiah would come and initiate them into the life of the Spirit. These people would find their security not in their status

121

as Abraham's children, nor in the ruses they adopted to ensure economic sufficiency, but in God's care. Thus the call to repentance is a call to end fruitless discussion of problems and to cease to despair of finding solutions while hanging on to what security we are able to find. It is a call to acknowledge God's judgement on wrong, and find security in the service of the King who sets things right and brings *shalom*, right relationships all round.

The biblical message of repentance is also a warning of judgement to give men time to repent. Jesus warned the elite in Jerusalem that their attitudes and behaviour would lead to their destruction, he saw it as inevitable. Confronted therefore with a manifest social injustice like the patterns of world trade, some radical Christians are calling men to repent in the following ways.

They are pointing out the injustice of world trade through statistics and moral evaluation. They are calling on people to acknowledge that the pattern of trade is wrong and that they profit by it wrongly. They are calling on people to submit to God's kingdom and express their repentance by paying the social cost of world goods. An American Christian economist, Norman Ewert, suggests that American Christians could pay three dollars a gallon for their petrol instead of one dollar (July 1979 prices), and send the extra two dollars for some form of development work. Christians will warn that such continual injustice in world trade asks for God's judgement and contains the seeds of its own destruction, in order that men may repent. They will work with all men of good will to propose and model alternative and just systems of trade.

Some may ask whether preaching repentance for involvement in social injustice leads men to personally commit their lives to Jesus. At a recent conference for the staff of World Vision in India (the U.S. based Christian relief agency) a speaker outlined areas of social injustice in India. At the altar call later that day six young social workers made personal commitments to Christ. Counselling revealed that the call to repent of social injustice showed them how relevant Jesus was. For how often do young men stop to ask themselves about loss of meaning in life, and how often each day do they profit from an unjust social system?

13: Counselling new christians

The desire to counsel and follow-up people who make personal commitments to obey and trust Jesus Christ marks effective evangelism. Counsel and follow-up usually takes place most successfully where there is continual contact between a Christian group and their new members. University churches with large influxes of students have special beginners' groups. City-wide campaigns sometimes establish groups of four to six weeks duration in different areas to link new Christians with people in their neighbourhood. When I belonged to the university Christian union and took part in counsellor and follow-up training for Billy Graham's visit in 1966, the syllabus for follow-up was fairly settled. New Christians needed assurance of salvation, and encouragement to read the Bible, pray and attend church.

Such a basic framework is still valid. But we have all been learning that more flexibility is necessary. Michael Harper writes:

> Although we are all destined to be changed into the image of Christ, the image from which we need to be changed will in every case be different, and the change demanded will be greater for some of us than for others. The changes may have to take place at a deep level. At the same time the world itself is in a constant flux, and we dare not ignore the considerable human, social and environmental influences on people, which can constitute serious hindrances to Christian maturing. There is a simplistic attitude, which needs to be firmly resisted, that Christian maturing has only to do with our 'spiritual lives', and provided that we are 'right with God' our maturity will be a matter of course. This subtle modern form of gnosticism is a

denial of our God-created humanity, for our spiritual life cannot be detached from our total being, which include our body, mind, spirit, emotions and environment.[1]

Others have richer experience from which to write about counselling new Christians. I can only record what people are learning and what radical discipleship requires. Michael Harper points out that maturing as Christians must cover the whole of our humanity and take the differences in our humanity seriously. Therefore whether in personal counselling, or in a group programme, we must be sensitive to the real person before us. A framework of topics in our mind may be a useful guide, but we may begin best with person-centred questions. 'What was it about Jesus Christ that excited you? What attracted or challenged you to commit yourself to him? What were you expecting or looking for? What changes do you think he will make in your life?' These questions will hopefully build many-sided conversations that open persons up to each other, and open up the whole of their life to Christ. We will not impose a structure on people; that would communicate that God is not sensitive to their individual personhood. But we will have a biblically informed goal of Christian maturity. The Nottingham Statement defines Christian maturity in these terms:

Becoming mature in Christ involves both the deepening of our relationship with him in repentance, faith and obedience and the transforming into his likeness, which will include our thinking, behaviour, attitudes, habits and character. Together with growth in the knowledge of God and his truth, there should be a development in capacity to distinguish between good and evil. The supreme glory of this maturing is the increasing ability to love and be loved in our relationship with God, the Church and the world. This transformation is accomplished by the action of the Holy Spirit, using the means of grace (worship, sacraments, prayer, preaching, Bible Study etc.).[2]

This definition reminds us that counselling and follow up is not an individual matter alone. Christians will grow to maturity in a group relationship where Christian fellowship is real. Individual personal attention has its place, but Christians are learning that fellowship is not a means to the end of their individual growth. It is in fellowship that we are to live. It is through fellowship that we experience some of the healing love of God which we need to heal deep personal hurts. It is through fellowship that we learn to serve and discover the gifts God has given us for the body of Christ.

Such fellowship may be provided in a special beginners' group. But this will only produce lasting results if other small groups exist in a church to welcome young Christians. Some churches form area fellowship groups, to build relationships between Christians in a neighbourhood. Two working class mums in Leeds who became Christians slowly learned their Christian life by joining a group of young Christian mums who met to talk and pray about bringing up their families. Occasionally the group held Bible study starting from some aspect of daily life.

The sort of leadership appropriate to this kind of Christian growth enables, rather than directs. Many who lead and teach in churches today exercise a parent-child form of leadership. The leader 'knows'. He passes on information to those who don't know. This 'information centred' approach in Christian education works well among students. They are used to experts, readily assimilate information and form attitudes based on cognitive learning techniques. They also bring their own well-articulated thoughts into dialogue with what they hear. So they actually contribute to the learning process. Though the pattern is 'parent-child' and 'information-centred' the quality of the listeners mitigates the worst effects. But when those listeners use this pattern to communicate Christian truth to non-intellectual audiences, the learning will not be so successful.

First, few people learn through cognitive information alone. When Bible studies are dry and academic, Christians rightly complain that they learn nothing. Secondly lay Christians do not take easily to leadership responsibilities in a 'parent-child' pattern of teaching. They are rightly shy about accepting the role of expert in this hierarchical model with respect to their fellow church members. We need to develop adult-adult leadership patterns that enable people to develop and learn together as a group.

Teaching radical discipleship is not just a matter of giving new content to six talks on 'Basic Christian Living'. It involves group learning together and a new approach to educative leadership. It also involves the life of the whole Christian community in passing on to new Christians what it knows of Christ.

14: The whole community teaches discipleship

Christian maturity covers the whole of our humanity. We often reduce Christian maturity to the 'spiritual' activities of regular prayer and Bible reading, personal evangelism, Christian service and active concern for missionary societies. We neglect goals and motives in career or job, attitudes to community and social issues, involvement with others in fellowship and sharing, the practice of hospitality and the care of the underprivileged.

Our narrowed vision then determines the nature of what happens in our church life. Church life is church-centred. Church teaching encourages people in religious activities and gives guidance on individual-sized problems. Individual moral decisions, guidance, sex and family life are areas where issues are fairly clear and individual responsibility reasonably obvious. But the larger problems of social justice are ignored in church life. No Christian perspective is given. Sermons exhort Christians to bear a witness in work and in society for justice. But few opportunities are given for Christians to hammer out these problems in their fellowship together.

It is not enough to inspire a few students and young people with concern for Christian social justice. We will not significantly influence a church by training a new generation of young people. For when these young people meet the pressures of promotion, marriage, mortgage, time for a family, and difficult decisions at work, they will take the same decisions as the church at large. Our training in radical discipleship must be aimed at adults to work out Christian options in the middle of these pressures and issues.

We need to rethink our concept of Christian teaching and training. We give the impression that real Christian education takes place at theological colleges or on special courses and not in the life of the local church. 'We need to rehabilitate the view that real normal Christian training happens in the local church,' writes Peter Lee.[1]

Is our training elitist? A vast gulf yawns between intelligent Christians who carry large responsibilities at work and Christian ministers in full time teaching ministry. Christian church teachers have access through college training to a body of supposedly 'Christian' knowledge which puts the average Christian at a disadvantage. He is always cast in the role of learner from the expert. But that expert knowledge is in Bible background and Christian doctrine rather than in Christian witness in work and society. The Christian minister is trained to communicate to those who are his inferiors – children, young people and students. He is not trained to be an enabler for a group of equals or superiors in his field. We need to develop ways of learning which draw on the resources of skilled lay people as part of a training team. Evangelism Explosion trains adults to train other adults to explain the gospel to adults. One church arranged a sharing session on marriage which included newly-weds and older married couples.

Where should this teaching and training happen? It is tempting to conduct it in extra meetings, in the Sunday evening or mid-week fellowship. But this excludes over 50 per cent of church members and probably 90 per cent of those with heavy responsibilities who want training. Can we not deliver the goods in our central gathering for worship, fellowship and teaching, the weekly service? The Protestant concept of worship has always insisted on teaching to inform worship. St. George's, Leeds, has experimented successfully with teaching in worship which involves lay leadership. The congregation meets for an hour of study in small groups led by two elders of the congregation. Topics and levels of study are graded. Then the whole congregation comes together for worship. Numbers at this morning

Christian Education Programme are increasing and other churches are observing and considering the experiment.

Why not develop possibilities in sermons and Bible expositions? A study group of informed people can meet with the presenter to discuss ideas and biblical insights on such subjects as 'bereavement' or 'work'. A preacher can end a sermon by asking the congregation to form groups of five or six to formulate a question, or comment, with which to respond. Few of these ideas are new in normal learning sessions in schools, universities or business seminars. But we are peculiarly resistant to using them in Christian learning.

People do not only learn by receiving new information. The sermon is not the only part of the service which teaches the Christian life. Some services begin with three minutes for people to meet their neighbours in the pew and teach the family life of the worshipping community. Churches teach God's creativity by hanging banners on the walls, or communicate his praise through colour or flowers. Services which encourage church members to take part in formal and informal ways teach every member ministry. Warm enthusiastic singing of old or new tunes with or without a choir, with an organ, guitars or small orchestra all communicate the vitality of God's praise. Churches which are not encumbered with pews try to express togetherness by arranging chairs in a hollow square or horse-shoe.

Everything cannot be done at once. In a cross-section of the population all such innovations together would probably alienate many established worshippers. Patterns popular in small young communities in Theological Colleges will not necessarily suit all local churches. But warmth, fellowship and participation are non-negotiable features of Christian worship. There is no defence for a service that is little more than a monologue sandwiched by hymns.

I have stressed the possibilities of the regular meeting for worship as a learning centre for a fellowship because we need to develop that concept. But other ways of learning can reinforce the central one. One London Church tackles current issues at an after-church 'Walking Parish Magazine'

—.an assortment of interviews, case-studies, dialogues and debates. Our church in Bangalore gathered all Christian businessmen after morning worship for a seminar and working lunch on 'Christian practice in corrupt business'. Out of the meeting emerged a plan to finance young Christians wanting to set up in business. In Leeds a discussion group on *Rich Christians in an Age of Hunger* decided to stretch resources by buying and renovating some old housing as a joint venture. They also gathered a salary to pay someone to educate churches in issues of international and local justice. In India, a women's fellowship invited the Food Price Officer to come and explain the rising food prices which were crippling so many. A Parochial Church Council could invite the city councillors for the parish to explain the problems of the area as they saw them.

These are essentially one-off meetings. A longer process of learning has developed in the Third World, called 'Theological Education by Extension'. Extension Education is widely used in South America, Africa, India and South East Asia among groups who are barely literate, up to degree level students. A report published by the Committee to Assist Ministry Education Overseas shows that 55,000 students in 77 countries are now studying through TEE. Between 1977 and 1980 numbers increased by 50 per cent. In the TEE programme in India, students use programmed material on their own for a week, and then come together to discuss with a tutor. Courses last for up to ten weeks. The basic material can be also used for a regular Bible Study where all can contribute, or as preparatory material for an intensive Saturday or Sunday conference. Programmed material greatly assists those who are not in the habit of studying through books and essays. Students come to the weekly group meetings with ideas to share and discuss arising out of the material. Many church members have strongly held opinions, which they have never exposed to informal Christian debate with others. The weekly meeting encourages discussion and interaction on some theme of Christian obedience. Here the study material delivers the group from excessive concentration on personal feelings, or pooling of ignorance. A TEE programme could provide excellent material for a fellowship group, or an all-age Sunday School. As adult education develops in the West and college training for Christian service becomes prohibitively expensive, we will probably see much training for Christian ministry in the West using TEE methods.

We need to use skilled lay people in training Christians to use their expertise in Christian witness in work and in society. Training will not be achieved by bringing a nationally known Christian business man to address a meeting, but by developing Christian business men together in a fellowship as Christian businessmen and managers.

The full time clergyman or elder will have to yield place so that others can develop. The full time leader of the congregation could begin to work in a team-role, continually yielding a place to others who have gifts for the whole body. In St. John's Church, Bangalore, we saw areas of ministry dramatically expand as two of us began to work closely as a team. We find that others now bring in their expertise for particular ministry with our team. Training for radical discipleship may begin as the leader of a fellowship begins to yield place to others so that the whole community can eventually take part in discipleship training.

15: How to do theology

In *The Christian Mind*, Harry Blamires laments that very few Christians approach everyday problems with a Christian mind. How can we train people to think confidently for themselves as Christians?

What prevents Christian people from thinking for themselves? Much Christian teaching creates false dependence on the pastor, on a few Christian authors, and on one tradition of interpreting the Scriptures. Could the reason be the way the teaching of the Bible is presented? People are encouraged to read the Bible for themselves but are also encouraged to get to know the message of the Scripture. This message is said to be one universal general message which is clothed in different ways in the Scriptures. Expert teachers are needed to unwrap this one message and apply it for people in different areas of life. The intellectual expert may be the pastor, the writer of their Scripture Union notes or their favourite author. But Christians leave the task of thinking Christianly for others to do for them. This becomes very obvious when Christians in one culture, say in India, import and reproduce without rethinking the books and theology of Western evangelicalism. But the same process takes place in evangelical circles in England.

We need to examine this model of Bible interpretation closely. This model says that the message of the Bible is (for example) that man is a sinner in rebellion against God, and of course this is true. But this general message is abstracted from the concrete particular descriptions of man's sin in the Bible. In the Bible, people sin by concrete disobedience to a known command of God (Adam), refusal to believe in Jesus and crucifying Him (the first-century Jews), worshipping the creature rather than the creator (cf.

Paul's letter to the Romans), organized social injustice (cf. Isaiah). By abstracting sin into a general message, *we lose the cutting edge of what Scripture says.*

Secondly: in abstracting sin into a general message *we pass what Scripture says through our cultural filters*. One cultural filter in the West is individualism. We see correctly that all men sin individually, but we have filtered out the corporate dimension of sin as injustice in society. Why have evangelical Bible believers overlooked the corporate aspect of social injustice in the prophets for so long? The process of getting at the message of the Bible has filtered out social sin.

Thirdly: in abstracting sin into a general message, *we read Scripture as a law code which sets out what we should and should not do*. We recognise that scripture is designed to shape our lifestyle, but we fail to read it first in its own particular cultural setting and appreciate the way God's word called men to obedience in their society. For example, in the parable of the good Samaritan we deduce the very familiar teaching that we should help someone in need. Not until we realize that Jews and Samaritans hated each other do we understand that the parable teaches the Jews an object lesson by holding up a Samaritan who helps a Jew as an example of love. It is like telling a Protestant audience in Northern Ireland of a good IRA man helping a wounded Protestant.

Fourthly, in applying the general message which we have abstracted through our cultural filters and without regard to the cultural reality of the Bible, *we make general, moralising, applications without letting the Scripture question the real issues in our culture*. Our cultural filters blunt the application of the Bible's message. The Bible tells us to love and help the poor and we apply this by giving money to charity. We don't let the Scripture ask us why people are poor in our culture, or our world. The Bible tells us to repent of our sin in order to commit ourselves to Christ. We apply this to sex and drugs. We fail to let the Scripture point out glaring sins we participate in and benefit from in society, such as patterns of international trade.

Bible reading becomes a task in which we intellectually appreciate God's word. But in the Bible we find that God's word called men to obey him. Our theology becomes an intellectual jigsaw to fit all the pieces of God's revelation into one universal message. But theology should be what results when each Christian and Christian community applies scripture to his life situation and works out what is true and relevant about God and his will for them today. The Christian educator should be like a midwife to enable a Christian community to do its thinking. He should not do the community's thinking for it. This model of Biblical interpretation in practice often cuts important corners. It delivers a pre-packed message which stifles creative Christian obedience in response to God's revealed authoritative word.

We need a number of correctives as we read the Scriptures. First we need to remember that both the Scripture and ourselves belong to particular cultures. Culture includes a society's world view – that point of reference which gives cohesion to abstract thought, social norms and economic structures. It explains why and how things exist, continue or change. It evaluates forms of social life and behaviour which are proper and improper. It gives psychological stability in times of crisis and gives sociological identity in times of peace. It systematises and orders the varied perceptions of reality in society into an overall perspective. It gives unified meaning to what happens in society. (This understanding is a précis of the model given by Charles Kraft in *Christianity in Culture*.[1]) Therefore we must understand the culture if we are to understand a message communicated in one society or if we are to communicate into another. Cultural conditioning is not an unfortunate accident which distorts human messages and words, it is a vital necessity for communication to take place. We communicate within the words and meanings of our culture.

The Bible is necessarily culturally conditioned. This does not mean that the understanding of God in the Bible merely arises out of a sociological process or contains mistakes or limitations because of its connection with its particular culture. It means that God communicated to Abraham, Moses, Isaiah and Paul in the language, meanings, and setting of their cultures. God communicated to them as real people in their own situations with his word for their time and place. He did not communicate with them only as symbolic representatives of universal men and women with a word which was chiefly applicable for later ages. In fact God's word speaks to us now because it first and primarily spoke to Abraham and Moses in their situation then. When Isaiah had a vision of God in the temple God appeared to him as a king, because Isaiah lived under a monarchy. The more we know of Israelite kings, the more we will understand what Isaiah learnt about God when he saw him as the true exalted King. Jesus defined his mission as the invasion of the kingdom of God, an idea full of meaning in the Jewish culture. Paul communicated the idea of God's rule invading the world in different terms which could be understood in the Greek society to which he was communicating. We need to appreciate the cultural setting of each part of Scripture in order to fully grasp its original meaning fully. For example, when David said 'The Lord is my shepherd', he did not only have in mind the picture of a caring and friendly pastoral uncle. The phrase would have had a similar meaning to the phrase 'My king', because shepherd was a term for the Israelite king. So we need a deeper acquaintance with the culture of the Scriptures. But, in doing so, we can find that our own cultural conditioning continues to affect us. To continue the example, in the United Kingdom we do not live in a monarchy as constituted in biblical times. 'The Lord is my king' is not a parallel expression to 'Queen Elizabeth is my queen'.

We are also culturally conditioned. Each culture is a way of viewing the world and society, with its own strengths and weaknesses. We think within the framework of our culture. The framework of our culture may hinder us from appreciating aspects of other cultures. For example, as an Englishman in India it took me some time to see the value of the custom whereby relatives, friends or acquaintances make a point of seeing a person off on a journey at the last point of departure or the first point of arrival (the railway station or the airport). It is estimated that at Delhi airport an average of four people come to greet or say farewell to a passenger. From thinking that such a custom is unnecessary, and discouraging friends from thinking that they had to take the time to do this for me, I am learning from experience that the custom plays an important psychological role in the process of travel in India.

We make judgements within the framework of our cultures. Sometimes the cultural pressures on these judgements are so strong and all-pervasive that we identify cultural assumptions about religious belief and morality with the teaching of the Bible. In earlier centuries it took many Christians decades to admit that the Bible did not require people to believe that the earth was flat. In later centuries many Christians took decades to accept that birth control conformed to a biblical understanding of sex relations. Today some Christians believe that the Bible teaches the inferiority of the black races. Our cultural conditioning makes us selective as we read the scriptures and can blind us to crucially relevant aspects of its message for our culture.

In translating into our cultures today the message which God communicated in the Biblical cultures, each generation needs to use the wisdom of past Christians, but needs to do the task afresh. No culture makes neutral judgements about human value. All cultures have strengths and weaknesses in their valuation of human beings. The translation of the scriptural message into terms relevant for one culture will be inappropriate in some aspects for another culture because it will fail to challenge some important misjudgement in it. For example, in the first three centuries of the Christian era, Christians discussed how Jesus could be God and man within the Greek cultural ideas of God and man. Their solution affirmed that Jesus was truly God and truly man but in terms that we do not now find natural – *hypostasis* and *homoousios*. Their solution challenged the prevailing concept that God was totally unconcerned with material created things and that man was, by his very existence, separated from the higher level of God. We would not preach this message today; but at the time, it was vitally relevant. Today, we need to affirm the full deity and humanity of Jesus. But we need to go back to the Scriptures and use scriptural teaching to challenge distortions in our own culture. If we merely reiterate the deity and humanity of Christ, we will lock him up in a religious box unrelated to political and social issues today. We will affirm that Jesus has no questions to ask of today's social and political order by which the rich get richer and the poor poorer. We need to read the Gospels afresh in the light of questions about the way modern economic culture disfigures humanity.

The Scripture is therefore not a collection of timeless truths which are universally applicable as they stand to all men. Neither are we neutral interpreters who can approach the text free of our cultural spectacles, or social biases. Our task is to affirm the objectivity and authority of the Scripture as God's inspired and authoritative revelation, but not identify that revelation with any one theological formulation of what the Scripture teaches. The Bible is authoritative revelation, but Christian books are not. Our task is also to interpret the Scriptures with relevance to each culture and situation and to acknowledge that our cultural filters, and the cultural filters of our hearers, play a part in that process, not as a barrier to interpretation but as a vehicle for it. So if our ministry is to interpret the Scriptures to people who are sick and seeking healing, we will properly select material from the Scriptures that speak to their condition and which may leave young healthy teenagers in the youth club cold.

The process of interpretation will find a helpful model in God's means of revealing himself in the incarnation. God revealed himself in a particular culture at a particular time in Jesus Christ. God took the Jewish culture and its social situation seriously, as we saw in chapters 3 and 11. Jesus, the Word of God, was incarnate in a particular context. He expressed his mission and his message in the terms of that context, he took sides, especially the side of the poor, and was committed to change the context. He made his meaning clear to his hearers, yet at the same time shattered many of their assumptions. He spoke of the Good Samaritan; he was the king who rode on a donkey, the master who was a servant.

In the incarnation, Jesus did not clothe a number of universal ideas such as love and brotherhood, which could be arrived at from other ways of thinking, in the realities of Palestine society. He was not making concessions to man's limited ways of thinking by putting universal abstract ideas in concrete form. He was actually revealing God and communicating the words and the works of God. The writer to the Hebrews sums it up in these words: 'In the past, God spoke to our ancestors many times and in many ways through the prophets, but in these last days he has spoken to us through his Son.' (Hebrews 1:1). In John 10:37–38 Jesus says: 'Do not believe me, then, if I am not doing the things my Father wants me to do. But if I do them, even though you do not believe me, you should at least believe my deeds, in order that you may know once and for all that the Father is in me and that I am in the Father.' The words and works of Jesus in his society are the revelation of God. God calls his people to share that revelation in the same way. In commissioning the disciples, Jesus said 'As the Father sent me, so send I you' (John 20:21).

The model of the incarnation will help us to decide the Bible's meaning by first *requiring us to examine Jesus closely in his complete context*. We must examine the social, economic, political and religious context of Palestine, and examine the stances that Jesus took in that context to reveal God's will and his purpose. We must read the Christian Scriptures from the central reference point of Jesus Christ, the carpenter of Nazareth. All the Old Testament points to the incarnate Lord, and the New Testament writings proceed from him. If we proceed from a non-incarnate Christ, our interpretation of the Bible will be abstract.

Secondly, the model of the incarnation will help us to decide the Bible's meaning by *calling us to see that the Bible can only be interpreted faithfully as to its intention by people who are committed to obey God in their contexts*, in the same style as Jesus was committed to obey God in his context. As Jesus himself said: 'Whoever is willing to do what God wants will know whether what I teach comes from God.' (John 7:17).

Thirdly, the incarnation reminds us that *the goal of Bible study is not to produce abstract theological truths and fit together a jigsaw of biblical doctrines*. The goal is to seek by word and deed to incarnate in our context the words and works of Jesus.

How could this model be used in an actual situation? If we were seeking the meaning of the Bible together in South Africa, we would have to study the stances that Jesus took on the issues of racial, social and economic divisions. We would engage in the study as we sought, as a Christian fellowship, to break down the barriers that were enforced between black and white and rich and poor in whatever way was open to us. Perhaps we might discover new richness in the biblical themes of forgiveness, loving enemies, overcoming distrust and fear, establishing just economic and social relationships, confronting the authorities, and suffering yet emerging victorious.

Such a way of interpreting Scripture would also help us to see that we can learn so much about the meaning of the Bible by reading what Christians in situations and countries different from ours find in it to help them. The richness of the meaning of the Bible will not be made clear to one group of people in one country and situation alone. We will all learn of the possibilities of the meanings of the Scriptures as we listen to people in other countries, and in other epochs of history, as they seek to listen to God's Word speak to them.

The point that Christians who are discussing radical discipleship are making about Bible study is that we cannot fully understand or interpret the Bible's meaning for us unless obedience in our context is a part of the process and a goal of the process. If obedience in the context is not part of the process we can mouth, debate and discuss what other people say the meaning of the Scripture is for *them*, but we will not be in a position to interpret its meaning for us. So

Jesus' call to lose our life for the gospel's sake will only be understood and interpreted by those who begin to commit their whole time and personality to Christ's cause in whatever work they do. This experience and activity of obedience to Jesus' call will in turn send them back to the Scriptures with new questions arising out of their experience of obedience.

There is, of course, much more to be said and discussed about interpreting the Bible and doing theology. Radical discipleship is offering this insight to the Christian community. It is not negating the traditional method of studying the Biblical text deductively: of beginning from Scripture, deducing principles for God's action in the world and the obedience he requires from his people, and then questioning our motives, our worldview and our behaviour. Nor is it in any way denying the objectivity of the authority of the Scripture with its record of the full deity and humanity of Christ, his atoning death, his bodily resurrection, and his presence by his Spirit in his Body, the Church. It is suggesting that we can be assisted in understanding the full meaning of God's acts of redemption in Jesus Christ for us today if we also proceed inductively. We can begin from the context we live in, the situations that face us in our lives, the choices we have to make in educating our children, the basis on which we decide whether our pay is fair, the ways in which we seek to play a responsible role in our neighbourhood. We can analyse these issues as far as possible into some basic principles, values, questions or options and then go with these issues to the Scriptures and ask how God's Word and the perspectives on man and society given in the Scriptures shed light on them.

Bible study groups that train people to think Christianly for themselves might adopt inductive procedure to discuss deprivation, compromise, affluence, security, identity, failure, housing, power, family life, sickness, community life and economic pressures.

There are two resources for doing theology – the Bible and experience. People need to come to the Bible with questions from their experience and come to their experiences with questions from the Bible. Christian education needs to enable people to carry on this two-way discussion within their own lives and within the Christian community to which they belong.

Nothing said in this chapter should be taken to detract in any way from a firm evangelical conviction in the full authority and inspiration of the Scriptures. What we should learn to question more often is our culture and our tradition of interpreting the Scriptures. Jesus made it clear that traditions could prevent men from understanding God's word.

16: Finding the Bible's meaning

The goal of interpreting the Bible is to find the meaning of the Scriptures for our obedience in our context. To achieve this goal radical discipleship starts with the objectivity of Scripture as God's authoritative Word to man with its record of the full deity and humanity of Jesus Christ, his ministry, his atoning death, his bodily resurrection and his presence by his Spirit in his Body, the Church. This guarantees its evangelical stance. Radical discipleship also affirms that the Scriptures have universal significance for all men, that they have the power of God to transform every situation, and that they are the means whereby all can experience the reality of God's grace and power.

In order to have meaning and power for every situation, Scripture must have meaning in each situation. We must begin by finding the meaning of Scripture in each situation for three reasons.

First, in the Bible, God revealed himself in both words and actions, calling men to obedience in specific situations. God's Word called Abraham to leave his own country, John the Baptist to preach to the tax-collectors about justice, and Paul to stop persecuting Christians and to serve the risen Jesus. In his actions of judgement and deliverance on the nation of Israel, God called his people to obedience.

Supremely, God revealed himself in the whole life of Jesus, in both his words and his works. God revealed himself in Jesus' lifestyle, his healing ministry, his social, economic and political stances in the society of Palestine, as well as in his words. We discover the meaning of God's revelation in Jesus by examining the whole life and ministry of Jesus in the whole context of Palestine, and its further interpretation in the life and obedience of the early church. For God's Word to bring life to the world, he became flesh in a particular situation and context. So we cannot find the meaning of God's revelation in Jesus in his words divorced from their setting. God's Word became flesh in Jesus.

Secondly, we find the meaning of God's Word for us as we engage Scripture with the whole of our own personal social, economic, political and religious context. In the western culture, Christians are tempted to make the personal and individual context primary, and the social context subservient to it, composed of the sum of individual contexts. This forces the Word of God to address the social context only through the grid of people's personal context. This appears to reverse the biblical pattern. Moses, the prophets, John the Baptist and Jesus began their message: 'Hear, O Israel!' They addressed their message, and took their actions, with reference to the situation in the nation as a whole. Their mission was to the people's whole situation. Their message had varied implications for different groups and individuals. For example, Jesus did not address the same condemnation to the poor as he did to the Pharisees. The fact that God addressed his people in their total context means that he addresses all men in their total context. For through his servants and his Son, God addressed Israel as a prototype of his true and just society. Israel was to be a light to the nations, God's model and pattern for a true human society.

The third reason for finding the meaning of Scripture in each situation is that the total contexts in which we are set differ from each other. The purpose of Scripture is that all people may experience the reality of the grace and power of God. The meaning of Scripture in each situation through which people may experience the reality of God's life will differ. Scripture's meaning cannot be captured in a single and uniform formulation without reference to the contexts in which men and women are set.

For example, the formulation 'Jesus is Lord' is meaningless without the background of the biblical context where the Lordship of the risen Jesus was affirmed as God's Lordship over against Caesar's Lordship. Paul writes: 'Even though there are many of these "gods" and "lords", yet there is for us only one God, the Father, who is the Creator of all things and through whom we live.' (I Cor. 8:5–6). Paul affirms Jesus' Lordship by contrasting and addressing it to other lords. In his day those lords were the Roman Emperors and false deities. In many parts of the world today, these lords are primarily evil spirits. In the secular consumer society, these lords are economic forces and material possessions. In some countries the lords are oppressive rulers. We distort the meaning of God's Word if we merely affirm the concept 'Jesus is Lord', and do not address other lords who claim our allegiance.

We also distort the meaning of God's Word to us if we try to transfer the meaning of Scripture in one context directly to another context without seeking its meaning afresh in the next context. For example, in western society, Jesus' Lordship is often affirmed against the background of personal loneliness, insignificance, lack of purpose and the slavery of drug abuse and permissive sex. Jesus is the Lord who sets a person free and gives him purpose. In India, the only group liable to those particular problems are young westernised middle class people in the cities. I sat in an Indian village listening to one such young person describe Jesus' Lordship in these terms. His hearers were a tightly knit village community of poor and exploited labourers. His words had no relevance to their situation. He was declaring an evangelical tradition, not the meaning of God's Word for the villagers.

Radical discipleship has arisen as Bible-believing Christians have been confronted with situations of injustice, powerlessness and deprivation. They have sought God's Word to transform the situations and the people trapped in them. They have gone back afresh to the Gospels. They have examined the lifestyle of Jesus in the socio-economic and political context of his time with the questions of injustice and maldistribution of resources which press on us. In the process, they have discovered a new depth of meaning in the Gospels which remained unplumbed as long as their readers had only individual or religious issues uppermost in their minds.

It is interesting to note that the proposers of radical discipleship have often come from very conservative evangelical backgrounds. For example, in the United States, some are graduates of Bob Jones University and the Moody Bible Institute. They are still evangelicals, but the meaning of God's Word in their contexts has forced them to become radical in their discipleship. They were not radical secularists by background who have forced Scripture through a radical grid.

It is also interesting to note that it was not the academic biblical scholars who raised the issues of biblical social justice from their study of the Gospels. Ordinary Christians raised these issues as they were forced to grapple in their Christian mission with the problems of poverty and powerlessness in their own and other societies, and with the meaning of God's Word for those situations.

The Scriptures and the context

How may we bring our context, and the questions that arise from it, to the Scriptures? The Scriptures are the important factor in this interaction. Their content determines the content of God's Word in all contexts. Our own context must never determine the content of God's Word. The context must never become the text. But our context plays a vital role in enabling the Scripture to have meaning for us. We must bring those issues and situations in our context which cry out for God's Word, God's judgement and redemption to the Scriptures. Issues of Christian lifestyle were raised in the seventies as Christians became aware of global poverty, diminishing resources, maldistribution of wealth, injustice and exploitation. They brought these issues to the Scriptures and asked what God's life-giving Word was for the situation. They did not begin with individual questions of how they could lose weight, whether they should get fit through jogging, or even whether and how they could beat the effects of inflation on the family budget.

They began with large issues of the context, and addressed those issues to the Scriptures. They asked inductively what the Scripture meant in the context of diminishing resources and maldistribution of wealth. Then they proceeded deductively to apply that meaning to the personal issues that arose out of the global issues. They addressed issues of personal spending, sharing resources in family and neighbourhood groups, and promoting justice in society. Christians therefore started cutting down their spending, not primarily because the cost of living was rising, but in response to world poverty which was bringing to their attention the scriptural teaching to do justice and share with the poor.

Of course, the interaction between Scripture and our context is a continuing process which is never complete. The way we view our context should alter as we expose our first set of questions to Scripture, discover the counter-questions of Scripture, and reformulate our questions afresh. We may begin with an acute awareness of the drug problem among a certain group of young people in the school where we teach. We begin to look for the roots of this problem in, among other causes, how and why these people are not finding fulfilment in life. We address our questions about fulfilment in life to the Scriptures and we find statements about fulfilment in Christ in servanthood, and in Christian reconciliation between separated groups. So we may then come back to our own view of the young people, and ask if we have been viewing them as a separate group, say of highly privileged students, or assuming that the goal they should have in life is success rather than servanthood. We may then discover more meaning in the call of the Scriptures to seek first the kingdom of God. Our concern may then be focussed, not just in a desire to bring them back to the conformity against which they have been rebelling, in the successful middle-class ghetto, but to challenge their priorities in life with a new form of fulfilment.

Bible study groups that train people to think Christianly for themselves might adopt inductive procedures to discover vital issues in their context which cry out for God's

Word, for example the issues of marriage, youth, employment, the homeless, loneliness, race and inflation. Then we could go back to the Scripture to seek the meaning of God's Word for these issues in the biblical context. Then we should proceed, deductively, to work out the meaning of God's Word for society, and the implications for our own lives.

If a group is studying a book in systematic fashion, it should avoid understanding and applying its message only to the individual and religious contexts of their lives. It should ask such questions as: 'What did this message or behaviour mean in the society of the day? What groups were especially challenged by this message? Who would oppose it and why? How did this behaviour conflict with accepted social norms?' In a study of Galatians, for example, the group should focus attention not only on the importance of justification by faith, but also on its social implications in reconciliation and fellowship across the social barriers between Jews and Gentiles. The group should examine what barriers exist between people in their own context, and how Paul's view of Christ's redemption addresses them.

Guarding the Faith

Proponents of radical discipleship have the confidence that when engaged with our situations, Scripture will not produce heresy. We preserve the integrity and purity of the faith once delivered to the saints by continually engaging the Scripture afresh with new situations. This is the evangelical heritage. Over the last hundred years, the key questions that challenged Christians in the western culture to seek the meaning of God's Word for their day were the questions of science, rationalism and scepticism. Evangelical Christians have been seeking to show that the deity, atonement, and bodily resurrection of Jesus Christ is actually the key to making sense of what rationalists portrayed as an impersonal and mechanistic world. The central doctrine of the Reformation, justification by faith, arose as Luther engaged the Scripture with the oppression of a church which made the individual's search for salvation a source of its own wealth, power and political control. Justification by faith not only lifted Luther's burden of guilt, it also undermined the oppressive rule of the medieval church. It was the basis for asserting that all believers were priests and could have direct access to the grace of God without the mediation of greedy officials.

In England in the eighteenth century, working children and the children of workers roamed wild on Sundays. The established churches had minimal contact with working people, and further believed that religion was too important a matter for children. Robert Raikes, a newspaper owner, sought to make the Scripture speak to the situation as he saw it, and founded the first Sunday Schools in 1780. Later the Children's Special Service Mission began its work. In the context of a disobedient church, dedicated Christians expressed their commitment to biblical faith by making it alive and relevant to children, and later to students through the Christian Unions. The Sunday Schools, the CSSM and the Student Christian Unions through the Inter-Varsity Fellowship, have been closely involved in the evangelical revival in the United Kingdom. They began with people who engaged the Scriptures with their context, rather than applying yesterday's scriptural answers to the questions of their day.

In the Bible itself, the faith is preserved as the Scriptures are made relevant to the context. In his letters, Paul urges Timothy to remain faithful to what he has received. He spells out what faithfulness will mean: avoid endless genealogies, warn the rich, care for widows, see to proper church order, follow Paul's own pattern of suffering and adhere to Scripture because it equips the man of God for every good work.

To guard the faith once delivered to the saints is therefore not the same as to defend it against the questions of the past, or state it in terms relevant to other contexts. That would be to ask yesterday's questions and someone else's questions of God's Word to us today. That would be to reaffirm yesterday's answers and give yesterday's obedience. It would be to replace obedience with legalism. We must seek our answers and give our obedience. We guard the faith and find God's will for us as we engage the Scriptures with our context to discover their meaning. Of course, our contexts are not sealed off from each other. We do not live in entirely separate and unrelated contexts. Each of our contexts is interrelated and belongs to the global context. So we must also hear and listen to the questions, insights and challenges that others bring from studying the Scriptures in their different contexts in both geographical space and historical time.

17: Commitment and action

Three Baptist pastors called on one American professor of ethics on the same day. All had been sacked by their churches with one day's notice. They had declared themselves to be in favour of the civil rights' movement. They could not understand why their churches seemed so opposed to their stance, when they had been preaching about Christian love for years. The professor gently asked each pastor to what extent, in addition to preaching about love, they had enabled their congregations to live as loving communities.

We learn Christian obedience through action. There is no need to call on people to act. We already act in many spheres. We need to reflect on our action and ask what commitment it represents. For example what commitment to the poor is represented by our lifestyle and spending levels? Or take this experience of a young journalist: 'I was out of work for only ten days, I, who could count the number of times I had been badly depressed on the fingers of one hand and still have enough fingers left with which to eat a biscuit, was horrified how easily and how quickly I became depressed. Unemployment dehumanises a person and we are all guilty of a crime by allowing it to happen. It is an evil and unacceptable face of capitalism. I used to have a smug middle class attitude: it couldn't happen to me. I understand a little more why God has put us on this earth to work and that a job for every person is a divine gift. We should not upset God's plan.' This journalist learnt through his experience that his previous actions had expressed a commitment which complacently allowed the crime of unemployment to go unchecked, which smugly thought unemployment could never happen to him, and which presumably regarded the unemployed as lazy shirkers.

His actions in his journalistic work will now express a different commitment as regards this unacceptable face of capitalism.

Our action flows from our commitment and our being. The concern is not for mindless activism, but action which authentically expresses genuine Christian discipleship. Christian being must be expressed in obedient action. We do not fully respond to God's word until we obey in action. Jesus did not give his disciples a new set of extra tasks which were uniquely and inherently Christian. That would have been legalistic externalism. He so motivated and directed them that they did everything differently. So the emphasis is to reflect on action we are already involved in and discover what commitments it represents. We may need to seek whether new action needs to be taken to authentically express this Christian being. For example a certain young chemist needs to reflect hard before he will progress in Christian discipleship. He works in a multinational drug company based in Scotland. I asked him what he knew or could do about the sales of overpriced and unnecessary drugs exported by his company to the Tnird World. He replied that he just sat in his office and did his job and didn't ask that sort of question.

We cannot assume that if we all sit in our offices, factories and homes and do our job efficiently, that the normal working of society will produce justice without any participation on our part. We cannot just let society roll on. In the international order the normal working of society has made rich nations richer and poor ones poorer. In England, inner-city blight, new ghettoes of immigrants, unjust distribution of resources have grown up even in the Welfare State. However, we cannot give detailed prescriptions for an instant solution. In *Crusade* magazine Beryl Bye confesses that the 'simple lifestyle' movement has run into the whole set of international economic problems of justice which cannot just be solved by supporting a child in the Third World. That is why I am relieved that Christian faith proceeds from the claim that God's purpose for redeeming his whole creation has been achieved in Christ. We do not have to produce a programme to overcome evil and save the world. We have to express the reality of Christ's victory now, where and how we can. We are called to respond in our situation to the light we have received. We are not to be over-worried if we try and then fail. We only learn what is right in obedient action. Much provision has been made by our Lord for failure in action (repentance and forgiveness) but not for failure to act ('Depart, I never knew you' see Matt. 7:23).

Involvement

Two fundamental questions in society are: Who produces what? and, How are the results to be distributed? Only 25 per cent of the working population of England is engaged in manufacturing industry and probably a far smaller percentage of Christians. We tend to think of Christian involvement as service and welfare. But service and welfare cannot begin until there is the basic wealth to distribute and share. Jesus and Paul were in this sense involved in creating wealth as carpenter and tentmaker. England's population is slowly having to realise that at present there is no growth in the economy. Christians will need to play a part in rehabilitating the dignity of producing wealth; and that means making goods and not merely making money. They will need to be involved in questions of justice, as to what is produced. Though it is more profitable to produce one Rolls-Royce for a luxury market than twenty mini-cars, it is more just to produce twenty mini-cars. And though it may be profitable to import raw materials cheap from Third World countries and sell them dear as manufactured products, there is no justice in this form of creating wealth. Christians will need to argue for justice in producing goods in the international order.

In this way Christians will be involved with people expressing a meaningful concern for social justice in the problems all are grappling with. Evangelicals have often directed their social involvement in charitable service towards the kind of people whose distress makes them least able to resist their advances. This is charity where the strong and superior eternally help and support the weak. We need to work more with people on the issue of who produces what, and how the results should be distributed.

Of course Christians are to be involved in service and welfare among disadvantaged people. The Christian community is called to take the side of poor and powerless people, to take the way of servanthood, to challenge vested interests, cross social barriers, build a new community of different social groups, call the privileged to repent of abuse of their privileges, and suffer rejection and defeat if necessary. We are called to this because this is precisely the option God took in human history to overcome evil and demonstrate the invasion of his kingdom. But we must express this option in a way that helps people grow into the full humanity that God wills for them, not in a way that keeps them falsely dependent. Many Christians complain that the Welfare State creates a population dependent on the State from cradle to grave; and yet Christian and evangelical social work can create exactly the same dependence.

Examples

The key preposition is 'with', not 'for'. We work with people for their development and for justice. This means we must know who people are and what their situation is. Jim Punton asked international study groups on The Urban Poor to find out the answers to these questions.

> In your context who are the poor? In what sense are they poor? Why are they poor? What is their place in your wider society? Who benefits from their being poor? In what areas do the poor have power? In what conflicts of values or interests are they caught up? What distinctive values, beliefs, prejudices, customs etc do they have? What of their housing? Their amenities? Health and hygiene? Life expectancy? Literacy? Schooling? Employment? How are they served by legal, economic, and political institutions? Is there social mobility? Loss of family ties? Marital breakdowns? Delinquency? Infant mortality? . . . What strengths can you identify? Which skills and attitudes do

you affirm? How is joy expressed? . . . Do you see areas of exploitation? Of squalor? Of degradation? Of humiliation? Of despair? Of resilience? . . . What wrong assumptions are made by well-meaning 'outsiders'?

Ron McMullen[1] suggests that a Christian group should try and build a community profile of the neighbourhood in which it is set. This would cover such things as population, history of the area, industry, employment, wealth, housing, health, education, ministry groups, social institutions, voting etc. Such a profile would enable a Christian group to develop a social awareness of its area. Such knowledge will be vital for some church decisions. A Leeds church had to decide whether to commit £50,000 to buying the freehold on its church hall in the city centre. In the face of world hunger this was a lot for the church to spend on itself. But as the church surveyed the area it realized that if the hall became a multi-storey car park the inner-city area and the community would lose the only hall in the area for playgrounds, meetings and social events. So as a community project the church bought the freehold on the hall.

Ron McMullen also suggests that a group of young people could engage in an action-research project in a neighbourhood. They could survey what jobs people get after leaving school, where the families (aunts, uncles etc) of each youth club member live, how land is used, road accidents in the area, where the young children play etc. Such research could form the basis of creative displays at the back of the church, stimulate people to ask why, and lead to further action to ameliorate some of the problems encountered.

In Bangalore a pastor presided over a group of professional social workers in slum areas. He abandoned the project because church members just sat in the pews looking on. So he coaxed the women of the church to spend one hour each week talking 'woman's talk' in the *bustees* with mothers there – about children, keeping the house clean, shopping, bills, making ends meet, familiar subjects which concealed Himalayan sized problems for women working eight hours a day on a building site. The ladies of the

Church saw these 'donkeys', as a leading Indian sociologist calls them, with new eyes and new compassion. And they told others.

Jim Punton asks a very comprehensive range of questions about activities which share friendship and name Jesus among a deprived community. His list should stimulate ideas.

1 *Residential* – opting to live as one of the poor making their context our own, sharing their lives and neighbourhoods, living in interpendence with them.

2 *Service* – supporting in the finding of homes, food, medical treatment, jobs, legal advice, marital and family counselling, language skills.

3 *Solidarity* – standing alongside in the struggle for justice, against racism, homelessness, poverty, wrongful imprisonment, exploitation.

4 *Awareness* – enabling an understanding of the needs of the neighbourhood and the reasons for its plight; assisting in finding needed resources to mobilize for change; training in basic skills and community development; encouraging self-respect and confidence.

5 *Visitation* – in homes, hospitals, prisons, shelters.

6 *Hospitality* – keeping open homes, entertaining, baby-sitting.

7 *Festivity* – creating street festivals, family celebrations, songs.

8 *Arts* – Through music, song, dance, video, film, local radio, street theatre, neighbourhood art, creativity.

9 *Cross-cultural activity* – bringing together different ethnic groups, youth and age.

10 *Involvement* – running necessary amenities such as laundrettes, eating houses, crisis centres.

11 *Cell groups* – home groups, base groups, cells in factories, groups in prisons (for friendship, celebration, prayer, Bible study, action planning).

12 *Discipling* – creating new churches, 'lay' education, training in leadership, scripture memorization.

13 *Residential communities* – households, networks of

households and varying communities sharing lives, possessions and commitment to each other and the neighbourhood.

14 *Renewal* – bringing new vision, vitality and direction to tired organisations and structures.

Jim Punton suggests that Christians should live among deprived communities. A lot of work needs to go into this. Young people and young marrieds could move into inner cities, at least until the problems of educating children become too pressing. To facilitate this, Christians may need to give to buy housing which would form the base for such a Christian community. John Root writes in *Third Way* (May 1979) that three Anglican churches in Dagenham could not find vicars. He suggested Christians further afield need to give to support churches in these areas so that clergy do not need to be tied down as church secretary, treasurer and caretaker as well as pastor. Clergy have to move into such areas with their families and Christian families are needed. But such areas have schools with low educational performance. John Root asks that Christians give support to church schools with the best possible staff and support. Despite the high unemployment rate among teachers many inner city schools in the seventies were under staffed. Churches from economically and socially privileged areas need to give adequate support to churches which minister in deprived areas. In addition John Root asks that Christians question and change the sort of society that produces segregated pockets of affluence and misery, where a large proportion of a city's population are expected to live in crowded housing, depressing environments, areas of high unemployment and low educational achievement.

Many non-christian groups already work in deprived areas and would greatly value support from committed, caring people. Residents' interests need safeguarding and representing where decisions are made. Involvement in community association, tenants' association, community relations group, housing society, works association, playgroups for children, a community news paper, are unglamorous but vital contributions to the life of a powerless community.

Margaret Clay was concerned as a Christian for families living in a deprived area of Leeds. She bought a house there and began a five year fight to get on the city council to do something constructive for the area. After her success in May 1978, she said 'We have got thoroughly involved in the issues which really concern people, such as damp and condensation in Council houses. We have tried to work alongside local residents building a campaign. I have achieved a reputation as a fighter and people believe I am on their side.' With her team of helpers Margaret knocked on the doors of ten thousand homes in her ward to get to know every family. Margaret is an active member of a charismatic evangelical Anglican church in the area, and church members have been involved in her work. Involvement that makes a difference is not easy and will not happen overnight. But Margaret Clay shows what can be done.

18: Action and reflection

'Denying the gospel by false teaching is something to which traditionally we have learnt to be sensitive; denying it by false practice is generally less attended to and yet by ignoring the areas of greatest need in our society we are doing just that.'[1] In our churches we need to encourage action and reflection to discover whether our practice is consistent with the gospel.

We need to encourage models of Christian community life that express the sharing and care which we seek to express in wider society. As we try out these models we can reflect on how adequately they express the gospel and address the real problems. For example Ron Sider[2] suggests that Christians adopt a graduated tithe of giving. After they establish a basic minimum for living they give 15, 20 or 30 per cent of the extra for God's work. The more their income increases above the basic minimum, the larger percentage they give. The church cannot urge rich nations to share even one per cent of their GNP if their members will not voluntarily share with the needy.

Some Christians are taking up vegetable gardening to produce food to add to the world's supply rather than import yet more from poor countries. Others fast once a week or have a meatless day. One Leeds group has established a food co-operative to stretch resources and provide good, well-priced food for old people and single-parent families. Sharing expensive family appliances such as washing machines and deep freezers, and running car pools, are projects which Christian groups have taken up to stretch resources and express fellowship in Christ.

When we reflect on these attempts to share we realize that we don't naturally open ourselves to such sharing because we fear that our hard-won possessions will get spoiled. How many horror stories have we heard from people who have loaned their homes to visitors. Fridges are broken, furniture is torn and wall-paper spoiled. But rather than retreat from such sharing we need to develop a greater sense of responsibility and care for one another. If I don't care enough for you to take care of the records you loan me, I don't care enough for you.

Other practical models demonstrate the reality of deprivation. One Bible Study group studied Amos and decided to put on a Rich Man Poor Man Dinner. At the dinner all 300 paid the same fee but a random ten per cent sat down to a four course meal while the rest stood around with bowls of rice. Talks and displays followed on the maldistribution of the world's food resources. Another model is suggested by the authors of *Hard Questions for Rich Christians* – a study and action guide on *Rich Christians in age of Hunger*.

The group may wish to list goods and services, houses, cars, colour televisions, carpets, furniture, hi-fi, holidays etc, that are advertised in magazines and on television and assess their priority in our spending. Then divide into two groups. One Group (Group A) about a quarter of the total, will play themselves, rich Christians in the affluent West: the other three quarters (Group B) will represent Christians from developing countries.

Group B should then ask group A to describe what material possessions they own, and the sort of things they spend their money on. Members of Group B may wish to describe what they own and how they spend their money in a developing country.

Group B should then ask Group A how, as Christians, they feel able to spend their wealth buying a particular item or service in the light of the physical and spiritual needs of their brothers and sisters around the world. The discussion might include questions like: (1) What determined the amount you decided to spend on your house and why did you pick a particular location? (2) What determines the amount you spend on your clothes, food, house furnishings, consumer goods? (3) Do you think your decisions should take account of need in a country like mine? (4) If so, will you now review the way you make these decisions? (5) What changes do you think will result?

At the end the whole group should consider the reasons advanced by the members of Group A for the way they spend their money. How convincing are these reasons? Do you think they would convince a Christian from a developing country that we were using our God-given wealth faithfully? What would the group answer if he or she said the group's spending mostly reflected their conformity to society, not a new life in Christ which resulted in a practical concern for the spiritual and physical needs of other people in God's world?[3]

Many role-plays show the patterns of social relationships between rich and poor. A role play with realism is the 'Plunge'. Participants are given £1 and told to exist in a city for twenty-four hours. They may not call on friends or use any connections. They may not stay in their homes. After their experience they come together to reflect on what life is like for those who are rootless in a big city. Where did they spend the night? How did police and others treat them? What did they resent most?

Reflection can take place on the structures within the church fellowship itself. How often do churches merely reproduce the groupings of society? Does the Womens' Fellowship ever meet with the Youth Fellowship? What do the young singles group know of the problems of married colleagues? Many resentments can spring up between these groups. Singles can think that marrieds leave all the church work to them, and marrieds can forget that single people have to cook their own meals when they get home, and perhaps look after ageing parents. Very constructive discussions take place when a womens' fellowship meets with the church youth group and each group talks frankly about one another.

Other groupings within the church could meet to reflect on the requirements of discipleship for teachers, salesmen, social workers, businessmen. These groupings could include many callings. They focus on the issues facing one particular group, to offer understanding, support and the opportunity for Christian reflection on what people are actually doing in society through their jobs. Amidst the pressures today we cannot assume that Christians will automatically deduce on their own from sermons what they should do in their home and work. A church group might come together to survey needs and opportunities for Christian service in the area. Another group might study homelessness: members might include a school leaver who decorates bed-sits for unmarried mums, a person who works in the Housing Department, and a Christian religious studies teacher who has begun to work out the Old Testament principles governing the use of scarce resources such as land and housing.

The group may discover what a Cambridge group of Christians found; pressure was being put on the council to sell a group of old streets for office development. If people knew about and made use of housing grants they could make these sound old houses into excellent clean homes for old people and young couples.

Guidance for school leavers and students about employment can be given in a 'careers day' using lay people. Our student group ran such a day using Christian careers advisers from the Polytechnic, local Council and Christians in representative jobs.

Reflection

Such action will feedback into a maturing Christian fellowship. People will support each other as they face the problems even if they disagree on many issues. Such fellowships will provide more incisive Bible Study, informed worship and dependent prayer. Notice how the Psalms draw heavily on the psalmists' experiences of difficulties, oppression and experiences of God's hand in a situation of oppression and injustice to develop praise and inform prayer. For example, Psalm 10:8 ff. reads (GNB):

> The wicked man hides himself in the villages,
>   waiting to murder innocent people.

He spies on his helpless victims:
  he waits in his hiding place like a lion.
He lies in wait for the poor;
  he catches them in his trap and drags them away.

The helpless victim lies crushed
  brute strength has defeated them.
The wicked man says to himself, 'God doesn't care!
  he has closed his eyes and will never see me!'

But you do see; you take notice of trouble and suffering
  and are always ready to help.

The Lord is king for ever and ever.
  those who worship other gods
  will vanish from his land.

You will listen, O Lord, to the prayers of the lowly;
  you will give them courage.
You will hear the cries of the oppressed and the
  orphans;
  you will judge in their favour,
  so that mortal men may cause terror no more.

Skills can be developed in enabling a group to develop
its own sense of fellowship and group support. Christians
can be arranged in a circle to enable members to address
one another and not be dominated by the speaker. A
speaker who comes to initiate discussion can ask for the
experiences of the members or put questions to them during
the talk. For instance a speaker on immigrant communities
can ask group members who have been abroad, lived abroad
or have immigrant colleagues to share experiences. A
speaker can end by asking the group to break into groups
to formulate questions, comments or plans.

The whole power of New Testament faith was that or-
dinary people felt they could know God for themselves.
Jewish scholars made them feel they were ignorant about
God. Jesus said they locked the door to the Kingdom of

heaven in people's faces. The promise of the new covenant was that each one would know the Lord. Jesus and the apostles made people feel they could learn about God, through God's Spirit and with his fellowship for themselves. Peter and other leaders were not super-scribes, who replaced the Jewish authorities as dispensers of the real truth. They were overseers and enablers of the work of God's Spirit among groups who loved and obeyed Jesus.

Group learning and reflection through discussion, action and support is important for radical discipleship. It avoids false dependence on a leader or expert which inhibits growth and action. Too often Christian meetings on social involvement are monologues by experts. These rarely result in action because the format of the meeting inhibits participation, discussion or self-reliance. People need to gain confidence that together and with God they have the ability to do something. That confidence must be fostered by the format of the group meeting itself. Group education must enable people to take greater charge of their lives, develop their consciousness of belonging to particular socio-economic groups and help them find ways to deal positively with the problems and distortions to which their group is subject. This is the conclusion of the British Council of Churches' report on Adult Education, *Growing Persons*.

When the group assembles for discussion it may not always be necessary for the vicar or curate to assume the role of chairman. He need not assume the role of expert or teacher. Christian ministers have often taken the role of external authority-figure and given directives to Christian people on what they should be doing in their work. But a person *outside* a situation cannot tell people *inside* a situation what to do. Their viewpoint cannot be the same. Indeed their contribution may be resented. The best authority on my situation and my interests is me. The growth of my moral decision-making powers depends on my making moral decisions. Many methods of Christian teaching have not encouraged Christian people to work out their own answers from a dialogue between their experience and the scriptures.

164

The Christian teacher can point to biblical principles, Christian ethical approaches and important questions. But the information, the detailed discussion, the decision-making must come from the Christian involved in the situation. The Christian teacher will be a creative member of the group which draws on the experience, information, questions and mistakes of all its members.

Kevin Shergold describes such non-directive leadership in these words:

> Non-directive leadership does not mean 'without direction'. Non-directive means not dictating or commanding and it has been described as 'the pattern of the suffering servant rather than the authoritarian dominator'.[4]

T. R. Batten writes

> The worker who uses the non-directive approach does not attempt to decide for people or to lead, guide or persuade them to accept any of his own specific conclusions about what is good for them. He tries to get them to decide for themselves what their needs are, what if anything they are willing to do to meet them and how they can best organise, plan and act to carry their project through. Thus he aims at stimulating the process of self-determination and self-help, and he values it for all the potential learning experiences which participation in this process provides. Our task is not to force our views on others uninvited, but to bring others face to face with God's word and its relevance to daily life, and then let the Holy Spirit do his work.

19: The cost of radical discipleship

The New Testament is a manual on suffering. Jesus described himself as the Son of Man who would be rejected and killed. He told his disciples they would share his baptism into suffering. The Christian rite of baptism initiates us into the way of the cross.

In the Sermon on the Mount, Jesus tells his followers they will suffer to see right prevail. In Luke he warns his disciples that the time between his departure and return will be marked by suffering for Christians. At the last supper in John's Gospel, Jesus tells his disciples that they will be hated as he is hated. In Acts, suffering is almost a prerequisite for the spread of the gospel. When persecution comes on the Jerusalem Church and the Christians scatter they become outcasts. And outcasts like the Samaritans welcome them and turn to Christ. In Romans, Paul reminds his hearers that to share Christ's glory we must share his sufferings. In the Corinthian correspondence Paul argues that suffering is the mark of genuine discipleship. He bears in his body the death of Jesus which brings life to others. In Philippians Paul desires to experience the power of Christ's resurrection through sharing in his sufferings. The writer to the Hebrews traces the history of the suffering of God's people in chapter eleven. Peter reminds his hearers that if they suffer for what is right the Spirit of glory and of God rests on them. In Revelation, John tells suffering Christians that their brothers overcame the devil 'by the blood of the Lamb and by the truth which they proclaimed; and they were willing to give up their lives and die' (Rev. 12:11).

Throughout the New Testament, the pattern of Jesus' death and resurrection is repeated in the lives of Christians who suffer in the process of bringing the resurrection life, truth and right relations of God's Kingdom. An international study group produced the following list of suggestions for Christians who were preparing to live under suffering.

(a) Teach and memorise the word of God.
(b) Know that Jesus will return to set up his Kingdom.
(c) Form small groups for prayer study and sharing.
(d) Memorise hymns.
(e) Warn new believers about suffering in store.
(f) Inform Christians about suffering in other churches, and pray.
(g) Develop close fellowship within the Church and learn to bear one another's burdens.
(h) Agree to think the very best of each person, no matter what rumour or gossip may be spoken by someone about them.
(i) Learn to love your enemies now.
(j) Keep up to date on the political situation.
(k) Know how to answer the questions of anti-Christian views.
(l) Live a simple-lifestyle now.
(m) Become a community that cares.

It is remarkable (but should not be) how closely these suggestions resemble the teaching of the New Testament for the normal fellowship life of the Christian community. These Christian communities knew there was a price to pay for confronting evil and injustice in order to bring the life of the kingdom. They knew they would have to pay it. The call to people, especially those in power, to repent, involves a price. John the Baptist paid a price for his message of repentance. Paul was hounded by the Jews when he called on them to repent for rejecting Jesus. The call to repentance exposes conflicts and vested interests in society. Martin Luther King writes of hidden tension caused by years of racial discrimination. 'Like a boil that can never be aired so long as it is covered up, but must be opened with all its ugliness to the natural medicines of air and light, injustice must be exposed, with all the tension its exposure creates, to the light of human conscience and the air of national opinion before it can be cured.'[1] Groups and individuals who benefit from present injustices will react sharply to those who question their position. For example in a situation of full employment in a Western country, blacks may have the worst jobs but have enough prosperity not to question the injustice. When unemployment rates go up and prosperity declines, the first to suffer are the black population. They now compete directly with white men for the same jobs. Those who question the automatic right of white men to those jobs and the high unemployment among black school leavers expose the injustice of the system. Harsh words will be used of them. In a local election a retiring mayor fully expected to be returned in his ward unopposed as a form of political reward. When a local vicar opposed him on grounds of democratic principle, amazing abuse was heard from pillars of the Church who belonged to the mayor's party.

A price is also involved in taking sides with the powerless and oppressed. Jesus paid that price when he identified with tax gatherers, prostitutes and outcasts. It means suffering the same handicaps as they suffer. Becoming involved in an issue of justice means taking sides with some people against others. It sounds strange to speak of conflict and enemies. But Jesus never said we would never have any enemies. He told us that we should love them, that we should seek their best interests and not use violence against them.

Jesus died because he exposed the social and religious oppression of the Jewish rulers and demonstrated that God's true standards contradicted all their posturing. Jesus died because he exposed evil and sin for what it was, man's total rejection of God's rule over him. The cross shows the conflict that exists between good and evil, right and wrong, justice and injustice, God and Satan. Jesus didn't evade that conflict. He showed that entering the conflict with the life of God's kingdom could mean suffering, rejection and defeat. But out of the cross came new life, victory over evil and the possibility of a new community of right relationships.

Radical discipleship takes suffering in a confrontation with evil seriously. That suffering may be the hard work needed to collect data and information about a prevailing injustice; it may be the frustration involved in trying to bring an injustice to the attention of a local authority or private company; it may be the necessity of taking non-violent resistant action to highlight a wrong – even something as simple as a continuous procession of prams over a busy roadway where local housewives want a pedestrian crossing and the council refuses to provide one. Radical discipleship takes seriously the gospel of the cross and resurrection. God's action of confronting evil and suffering the consequences is the only method he has endorsed for defeating evil in the world.

These tensions and conflicts will not only arise between the Church and the world. They will also arise within the church. 'There were almost violent reactions when our large Christian nucleus in the Youth Club started to come to church in jeans and T-Shirts' writes one youth leader. Attempts to expose injustice and corruption in a large Christian organisation in the Third World were met by threats, court orders, and intimidation.

One college lecturer stated that conflict and confrontation were not appropriate in a Christian community. It would be more accurate to say that there is often acute conflict and confrontation hidden by silence and held in check by the powers that be. The question is, how do we handle such conflict? We should not pretend that there is agreement where none in fact exists. We should not force a powerless group to agree. We should seek reconciliation which means we must first get at the roots of the conflict, recognise them, repent where necessary and seek peace and healing.

Christian right relationships with God and between men were not bought cheap by Christ and cannot be bought cheap by his followers. Repentance means recognizing evil, wrong, sin and conflict for what it is.

Christian action and suffering will rarely be dramatic. It is often insignificant. We suffer from two thousand years of Christian history. The Christian faith and history of the Church loom large as we look back across the centuries or around our cities. Augustine and Canterbury Cathedral, Luther and the Reformation, John Wesley and the Methodist Revival, people, buildings and movements, give the impression that Jesus is important in worldly terms. But we mistake historical importance for contemporary significance. In their time, relatively few noticed Augustine, Luther or Wesley. To be effective as Christians in today's world we do not necessarily need to influence the impressive and important.

Jesus was insignificant in his day even in his tin-pot country. Israel counted for nothing in the politics of the Roman Empire; it was just another province. Jesus was a crank in the popular mind; he was a nobody who ended up on the wrong side of the authorities. Even monotheistic Jews who shared his views on God and the world found him incredible. He claimed that he was God's agent, and that his healing miracles and meals with law-breakers represented the invasion of all that was wrong with the world by the mighty kingdom of God. How could this solve any of the problems of the day?

Put Jesus in a similar situation today. Hear the voice of the oppressed represented in a speech at the Nairobi Assembly of the World Council of Churches in 1975. 'You are not the one for whom we wait. We need a God of power and you are weak. We need a leader with wide appeal, and you are a small town boy. We need someone to challenge Herod, and you concern yourself with fishermen.' Jesus was insignificant in worldly terms and he was crucified. But he told the parable of the mustard seed. The mustard seed is insignificant. Lose it in the earth and it dies. Place a chest of gold blocks in the ground alongside the mustard seed. The box of gold bricks will be photographed and then guarded by security police. The mustard seed will never be noticed.

But the mustard seed has within it the power of God. It springs to life and produces a tree that the birds of the air, the nations of the world will be glad to shelter in. The chest of gold will remain forever what it is.

The challenge of radical discipleship is whether we believe that God's kingdom is active in the world today, however insignificant it may appear in terms that the media can measure. Do we really believe that as we live the life-styles and ask the questions of the kingdom of God in our politics, economics, work and social life, God's power for change is breaking in? This is what the Christian faith asks its adherents to believe. Lord help our unbelief.

Appendices

The concern for a book on Radical Discipleship arose from a statement on Radical Discipleship produced at the Lausanne Congress on World Evangelisation in 1974. To appreciate the issues on which Radical Discipleship raises important questions, we reproduce (1) The statement on radical discipleship; (2) The Lausanne Covenant; (3) The Madras Declaration on Evangelical Social Action produced at the All India Conference on Evangelical Social Action in Madras in October 1979 (which reflects much of the thinking on Radical Discipleship).

Appendix 1
The statement on radical discipleship

The statement on Radical Discipleship was produced at the Lausanne Congress on World Evangelisation 1974. This was not an official Lausanne document. It was drafted and circulated by a group of participants in the Congress and was welcomed by those responsible for the drafting of the Lausanne Covenant, as an addendum to it. It is entitled *Theology and implications of radical discipleship*.

The Spirit of the Lord is upon Me
because he has anointed Me—
to proclaim good news to the poor:
He has sent Me to herald
liberation for captives and
recovery of sight for the blind,
to give freedom to those who are oppressed.

Luke 4:18

As the Father has sent me, so I am sending
you.

John 20:21

God is making known the good news:
Shalom through Jesus, He is Lord of all.

Acts 10:36

God was well pleased through Him to
reconcile the whole universe back to
Himself, making shalom through the
blood of His cross.

Col. 1:20

A number of issues have thrust themselves upon us from papers
delivered in this Congress and, from the subsequent wrestling
with them under the authority of God's word, a number of us
have felt the compulsion of his Spirit to share this response.

WE AFFIRM THAT . . . The *evangel* is God's Good News in Jesus
Christ; it is Good News of the reign he proclaimed and embodies;
of God's mission of love to restore the world to wholeness through
the Cross of Christ and him alone; of his victory over the demonic
powers of destruction and death; of his Lordship over the entire
universe; it is good news of a new creation, a new humanity, a
new birth through him by his life-giving Spirit; of the gifts of the
messianic reign contained in Jesus and mediated through him by
his Spirit; of the charismatic community empowered to embody
his reign of shalom here and now before the whole creation and
make his Good News seen and known. It is Good News of liberation, of restoration, of wholeness, and of salvation that is personal, social, global and cosmic. Jesus is Lord! Alleluia! Let the
earth hear his voice!

The *communication of the evangel* in its fulness to every person
worldwide is a mandate of the Lord Jesus to his community.
There is no biblical dichotomy between the Word spoken and the
Word made visible in the lives of God's people. Men will look as
they listen and what they see must be at one with what they hear.
The Christian community must chatter, discuss and proclaim the
Gospel; it must express the Gospel in its life as the New Society,
in its prophetic exposing and opposing of all demonic forces that
deny the Lordship of Christ and keep men less than fully human;
in its pursuit of real justice for all men; in its responsible and
caring trusteeship of God's creation and its resources.

173

There are times when our communication may be by attitude and action only, and times when the spoken Word will stand alone; but we must repudiate as demonic the attempt to drive a wedge between evangelism and social action.

The *response demanded by the evangel* is that men and women repent of their sin and every other lordship than that of Jesus Christ, and commit themselves to him to serve him in the world. Men are not already reconciled to God and simply awaiting the realisation of it. Nor can biblical authority be found for the false hope of universalism; the reality of the eternal destruction of evil and all who cling to it must be solemnly affirmed, however humbly agnostic the Bible requires us to be about its nature.

Salvation is by God's grace on the sole ground of Christ's atoning death and resurrection and is received by obedient faith. Repentance is demanded; men must experience a change of understanding, attitude and orientation. But the new birth is not merely a subjective experience of forgiveness. It is a placement within the messianic community, God's new order which exists as a sign of God's reign to be consummated at the end of the age.

Methods in evangelisation must centre in Jesus Christ who took our humanity, our frailty, our death and gave himself in suffering servanthood for others. He sends his community into the world, as the Father sent him, to identify and agonize with men, to renounce status and demonic power, and to give itself in selfless service of others for God. Those who proclaim the Cross must be continually marked by the Cross. With unashamed commitment to Jesus Christ we must engage in the mutual listening of dialogue, the reward of which is understanding. We need to meet men on their own ground and be particularly attentive to the powerless. We must use the language, thought forms and imagery appropriate to differing cultures. As Christians, we must live in such unity and love that men may believe. We must allow God to make visible in the new humanity the quality of life that reflects Christ and demonstrates his reign. We must respect cultural integrity while being free from all that denies or distorts the Lordship of Christ. God's Spirit overcomes all barriers of race, colour and culture.

Strategy for world evangelization in our generation is with God, from whom we eagerly anticipate the renewal of his community, equipping us with love and power so that the whole Christian community may make known the whole Gospel to the whole man throughout the whole world. We believe God to be calling us into

174

greater unity and partnership throughout the earth to fulfil the commission of our Lord Jesus Christ.

WE CONFESS THAT . . . We have been failing in our obedience to the Lordship of Christ and have been refusing to submit to his word and be led by his Spirit.

We have failed to incarnate the gospel and to come to men as servants for Christ's sake.

Our testimony has often been marred by triumphalism and arrogance, by lack of faith in God and by diminished love for his people.

We have often been in bondage to a particular culture and sought to spread it in the name of Jesus.

We have not been aware of when we have debased and distorted the gospel by acceptance of a contrary value system.

We have been partisan in our condemnation of totalitarianism and violence and have failed to condemn societal and institutionalised sin, especially that of racism.

We have sometimes so identified ourselves with particular political systems that the Gospel has been compromised and the prophetic voice muted.

We have frequently denied the rights and neglected the cries of the underprivileged and those struggling for freedom and justice.

We have often separated Jesus Christ the Saviour from Jesus Christ the Lord.

We have sometimes distorted the biblical understanding of man as a total being and have courted an unbiblical dualism.

We have insulated new Christians from life in the world and given simplistic responses to complex problems.

We have sometimes manipulated our message, used pressure techniques and been unduly pre-occupied with statistics.

We have allowed eagerness for quantitative growth to render us silent about the whole counsel of God. We have been usurping God's Holy Spirit of love and power.

WE REJOICE . . . In our membership by his Spirit in the Body of Christ and in the joy and love he has given us in each other.

In the openness and honesty with which we have met each other and have experienced mutual acceptance and forgiveness.

In the possibilities for men to read his Word in their own languages through indigenous translations.

In the stimulation of mind and challenge to action that has come to us from his word as we have placed the needs of our generation under its judgement and light.

In the prophetic voices of our brothers and sisters in this Congress, with whom we go forth in humility and hope.

In the certainty that the kingdoms of this world shall become the Kingdom of our God and of his Christ. He shall reign forever, Alleluia!

WE RESOLVE . . . to submit ourselves afresh to the Word of God and to the leading of his Spirit, to pray and work together for the renewal of his community as the expression of his reign, to participate in God's mission to his world in our generation, showing forth Jesus as Lord and Saviour, and calling on all men everywhere to repent, to submit to his Lordship, to know his salvation, to identify in him with the oppressed and work for the liberation of all men and women in his name.

LET THE EARTH HEAR HIS VOICE!

From J. D. Douglas (ed.), *Let The Earth Hear His Voice* (World Wide Publications, 1975) p. 1294-96.

Appendix 2: The Lausanne Covenant

Introduction

We, members of the Church of Jesus Christ, from more than 150 nations, participants in the International Congress on World Evangelization at Lausanne, praise God for his great salvation and rejoice in the fellowship he has given us with himself and with each other. We are deeply stirred by what God is doing in our day, moved to penitence by our failures and challenged by the unfinished task of evangelization. We believe the gospel is God's good news for the whole world, and we are determined by his grace to obey Christ's commission to proclaim it to all mankind and to make disciples of every nation. We desire, therefore, to affirm our faith and our resolve, and to make public our covenant.

1. The Purpose of God

We affirm our belief in the one eternal God, Creator and Lord of the world, Father, Son and Holy Spirit, who governs all things

176

according to the purpose of his will. He has been calling out from the world a people for himself, and sending his people back into the world to be his servants and his witnesses, for the extension of his kingdom, the building up of Christ's body, and the glory of his name. We confess with shame that we have often denied our calling and failed in our mission, by becoming conformed to the world or by withdrawing from it. Yet we rejoice that even when borne by earthen vessels the Gospel is still a precious treasure. To the task of making that treasure known in the power of the Holy Spirit we desire to dedicate ourselves anew.

(Isa. 40:28; Matt. 28:19; Eph. 1:11; Acts 15:14; John 17:6, 18; Eph. 4:12; I Cor. 5:10; Rom. 12:2; II Cor. 4:7)

2. *The Authority and Power of the Bible*

We affirm the divine inspiration, truthfulness and authority of both Old and New Testament Scriptures in their entirety as the only written Word of God, without error in all that it affirms, and the only infallible rule of faith and practice. We also affirm the power of God's word to accomplish his purpose of salvation. The message of the Bible is addressed to all mankind. For God's revelation in Christ and in Scripture is unchangeable. Through it the Holy Spirit still speaks today. He illumines the minds of God's people in every culture to perceive its truth freshly through their own eyes and thus discloses to the whole church ever more of the many-coloured wisdom of God.

(II Tim. 3:16; II Pet. 1:21; John 10:35; Isa. 55:11; I Cor. 1:21; Rom. 1:16; Matt. 5:17, 18; Jude 3; Eph. 1:17, 18; 3:10, 18)

3. *The Uniqueness and Universality of Christ*

We affirm that there is only one Saviour and only one Gospel, although there is a wide diversity of evangelistic approaches. We recognize that all men have some knowledge of God through his general revelation in nature. But we deny that this can save, for men suppress the truth by their unrighteousness. We also reject as derogatory to Christ and the gospel every kind of syncretism and dialogue which implies that Christ speaks equally through all religions and ideologies. Jesus Christ, being himself the only God-man, who gave himself as the only ransom for sinners, is the only mediator between God and man. There is no other name by which we must be saved. All men are perishing because of sin, but God loves all men, not wishing that any should perish but that all should repent. Yet those who reject Christ repudiate the joy of salvation and condemn themselves to eternal separation from God. To proclaim Jesus as 'the Saviour of the world' is not to affirm that all men are either automatically or ultimately saved, still less to affirm that all religions offer salvation in Christ. Rather it is to proclaim God's love for a world of sinners and to invite all men to respond to him as Saviour and Lord in the wholehearted personal commitment of repentance and faith. Jesus Christ has been exalted above every other name; we long for the day when every knee shall bow to him and every tongue shall confess him Lord.

(Gal. 1:6–9; Rom. 1:18–32; I Tim. 2:5–6; Acts 4:12; John 3:16–19; II Pet. 3:9; II Thess. 1:7–9; John 4:42; Matt. 11:28; Eph. 1:20, 21; Phil. 2:9–11)

4. The Nature of Evangelism

To evangelize is to spread the good news that Jesus Christ died for our sins and was raised from the dead according to the Scriptures, and that as the reigning Lord he now offers the forgiveness of sins and the liberating gift of the Spirit to all who repent and believe. Our Christian presence in the world is indispensable to evangelism, and so is that kind of dialogue whose purpose is to listen sensitively in order to understand. But evangelism itself is the proclamation of the historical, biblical Christ as Saviour and Lord, with a view to persuading people to come to him personally and so be reconciled to God. In issuing the gospel invitation we have no liberty to conceal the cost of discipleship. Jesus still calls all who would follow him to deny themselves, take up their cross, and identify themselves with his new community. The results of evangelism include obedience to Christ, incorporation into his church and responsible service in the world.

(I Cor. 15:3, 4; Acts 2:32–39; John 20:21; I Cor. 1:23; II Cor. 4:5; 5:11, 20; Luke 14:25–33; Mark 8:34; Acts 2:40, 47; Mark 10:43–45).

5. Christian Social Responsibility

We affirm that God is both the Creator and the Judge of all men. We therefore should share his concern for justice and reconciliation throughout human society and for the liberation of men from every kind of oppression. Because mankind is made in the image of God, every person, regardless of race, religion, colour, culture, class, sex, or age, has an intrinsic dignity because of which he should be respected and served, not exploited. Here too we express

178

penitence both for our neglect and for having sometimes regarded evangelism and social concern as mutually exclusive. Although reconciliation with man is not reconciliation with God, nor is social action evangelism, nor is political liberation salvation, nevertheless we affirm that evangelism and socio-political involvement are both part of our Christian duty. For both are necessary expressions of our doctrines of God and man, our love for our neighbour and our obedience to Jesus Christ. The message of salvation implies also a message of judgment upon every form of alienation, oppression and discrimination, and we should not be afraid to denounce evil and injustice wherever they exist. When people receive Christ they are born again into his kingdom and must seek not only to exhibit but also to spread its righteousness in the midst of an unrighteous world. The salvation we claim should be transforming us in the totality of our personal and social responsibilities. Faith without works is dead.

(Acts 17:26, 31; Gen. 18:25; Isa. 1:17; Psa. 45:7; Gen. 1:26, 27; Jas. 3:9; Lev. 19:18; Luke 6:27, 35; Jas. 2:14–26; John 3:3, 5; Matt. 5:20; 6:33; II Cor. 3:18; Jas. 2:20).

6. *The Church and Evangelism*

We affirm that Christ sends his redeemed people into the world as the Father sent him and that this calls for a similar deep and costly penetration of the world. We need to break out of our ecclesiastical ghettos and permeate non-Christian society. In the church's mission of sacrificial service evangelism is primary. World evangelization requires the whole church to take the whole gospel to the whole world. The church is at the very centre of God's cosmic purpose and is his appointed means of spreading the Gospel. But a church which preaches the Cross must itself be marked by the Cross. It becomes a stumbling block to evangelism when it betrays the Gospel or lacks a living faith in God, a genuine love for people, or scrupulous honesty in all things including promotion and finance. The church is the community of God's people rather than an institution, and must not be identified with any particular culture, social or political system, or human ideology.

(John 17:28; 20:21; Matt. 28:19, 20; Acts 1:8; 20:27; Eph. 1:9, 10; 3:9–11; Gal. 6:14, 17; II Cor. 6:3, 4; II Tim. 2:19–21; Phil. 1:27).

7. Cooperation in Evangelism

We affirm that the church's visible unity in truth is God's purpose. Evangelism also summons us to unity, because our oneness strengthens our witness, just as our disunity undermines our Gospel of reconciliation. We recognize, however, that our organizational unity may take many forms and does not necessarily forward evangelism. Yet we who share the same biblical faith should be closely united in fellowship, work and witness. We confess that our testimony has sometimes been marred by sinful individualism and needless duplication. We pledge ourselves to seek a deeper unity in truth, worship, holiness and mission. We urge the development of regional and functional cooperation for the furtherance of the church's mission, for strategic planning, for mutual encouragement, and for the sharing of resources and experience.
(John 17:21, 23; Eph. 4:3, 4; John 13:35; Phil. 1:27; John 17:11-23)

8. Churches in Evangelical Partnership

We rejoice that a new missionary era has dawned. The dominant role of western missions is fast disappearing. God is raising up from the younger churches a great new resource for world evangelization, and is thus demonstrating that the responsibility to evangelize belongs to the whole body of Christ. All churches should therefore be asking God and themselves what they should be doing both to reach their own area and to send missionaries to other parts of the world. A re-evaluation of our missionary responsibility and role should be continuous. Thus a growing partnership of churches will develop and the universal character of Christ's church will be more clearly exhibited. We also thank God for agencies which labour in Bible translation, theological education, the mass media, Christian literature, evangelism, missions, church renewal and other specialist fields. They too should engage in constant self-examination to evaluate their effectiveness as part of the Church's mission.
(Rom. 1:8; Phil. 1:5; 4:15; Acts 13:1-3; I Thess. 1:6-8)

9. The Urgency of the Evangelistic Task

More than 2,700 million people, which is more than two-thirds of mankind, have yet to be evangelized. We are ashamed that so many have been neglected; it is a standing rebuke to us and to the whole church. There is now, however, in many parts of the world an unprecedented receptivity to the Lord Jesus Christ. We are convinced that this is the time for churches and para-church agencies to pray earnestly for the salvation of the unreached and to launch new efforts to achieve world evangelization. A reduction of foreign missionaries and money in an evangelized country may sometimes be necessary to facilitate the national church's growth in self-reliance and to release resources for unevangelized areas. Missionaries should flow ever more freely from and to all six continents in a spirit of humble service. The goal should be, by all available means and at the earliest possible time, that every person will have the opportunity to hear, understand, and receive the good news. We cannot hope to attain this goal without sacrifice. All of us are shocked by the poverty of millions and disturbed by the injustices which cause it. Those of us who live in affluent circumstances accept our duty to develop a simple life-style in order to contribute more generously to both relief and evangelism.

(John 9:4; Matt. 9:35–38; Rom. 9:1–3; I Cor. 9:19–23; Mark 16:15; Isa. 58:6, 7; Jas. 1:27; 2:1–9; Matt. 25:31–46; Acts 2:44, 45; 4:34, 35)

10. Evangelism and Culture

The development of strategies for world evangelization calls for imaginative pioneering methods. Under God, the result will be the rise of churches deeply rooted in Christ and closely related to their culture. Culture must always be tested and judged by Scripture. Because man is God's creature, some of his culture is rich in beauty and goodness. Because he is fallen, all of it is tainted with sin and some of it is demonic. The Gospel does not presuppose the superiority of any culture to another, but evaluates all cultures according to its own criteria of truth and righteousness, and insists on moral absolutes in every culture. Missions have all too frequently exported with the gospel an alien culture, and churches have sometimes been in bondage to culture rather than to the Scripture. Christ's evangelists must humbly seek to empty themselves of all but their personal authenticity in order to transform and enrich culture, all for the glory of God.

(Mark 7:8, 9, 13; Gen. 4:21, 22; I Cor. 9:19–23; Phil. 2:5–7; II Cor. 4:5)

11. Education and Leadership

We confess that we have sometimes pursued church growth at the expense of church depth, and divorced evangelism from Christian nurture. We also acknowledge that some of our missions have been too slow to equip and encourage national leaders to assume their rightful responsibilities. Yet we are committed to indigenous principles, and long that every church will have national leaders who manifest a Christian style of leadership in terms not of domination but of service. We recognize that there is a great need to improve theological education, especially for church leaders. In every nation and culture there should be an effective training programme for pastors and laymen in doctrine, discipleship, evangelism, nurture and service. Such training programmes should not rely on any stereotyped methodology but should be developed by creative local initiatives according to biblical standards.

(Col. 1:27, 28; Acts 14:23; Tit. 1:5, 9; Mark 10:42–45; Eph. 4:11, 12)

12. Spiritual Conflict

We believe that we are engaged in constant spiritual warfare with the principalities and powers of evil, who are seeking to overthrow the church and frustrate its task of world evangelization. We know our need to equip ourselves with God's armour and to fight this battle with the spiritual weapons of truth and prayer. For we detect the activity of our enemy, not only in false ideologies outside the church, but also inside it in false gospels which twist Scripture and put man in the place of God. We need both watchfulness and discernment to safeguard the biblical Gospel. We acknowledge that we ourselves are not immune to worldliness of thought and action, that is, to a surrender to secularism. For example, although careful studies of church growth, both numerical and spiritual, are right and valuable, we have sometimes neglected them. At other times, desirous to ensure a response to the gospel, we have compromised our message, manipulated our hearers through pressure techniques, and become unduly preoccupied with statistics or even dishonest in our use of them. All this is worldly. The church must be in the world; the world must not be in the church.

(Eph. 6:12; II Cor. 4:3, 4; Eph. 6:11, 13–18; II Cor. 10:3–5; I John 2:18–26; 4:1–3; Gal. 1:6–9; II Cor. 2:17; 4:2; John 17:15)

13. Freedom and Persecution

It is the God-appointed duty of every government to secure conditions of peace, justice and liberty in which the church may obey God, serve the Lord Christ, and preach the gospel without interference. We therefore pray for the leaders of the nations and call upon them to guarantee freedom of thought and conscience, and freedom to practise and propagate religion in accordance with the will of God and as set forth in The Universal Declaration of Human Rights. We also express our deep concern for all who have been unjustly imprisoned, and especially for our brethren who are suffering for their testimony to the Lord Jesus. We promise to pray and work for their freedom. At the same time we refuse to be intimidated by their fate. God helping us, we too will seek to stand against injustice and to remain faithful to the Gospel, whatever the cost. We do not forget the warnings of Jesus that persecution is inevitable.

(I Tim. 1:1–4; Acts 4:19; 5:29; Col. 3:24; Heb. 13:1–3; Luke 4:18; Gal. 5:11; 6:12; Matt. 5:10–12; John 15:18–21)

14. The Power of the Holy Spirit

We believe in the power of the Holy Spirit. The Father sent his Spirit to bear witness to his Son; without his witness ours is futile. Conviction of sin, faith in Christ, new birth and Christian growth are all his work. Further, the Holy Spirit is a missionary spirit; thus evangelism should arise spontaneously from a Spirit-filled church. A church that is not a missionary church is contradicting itself and quenching the Spirit. Worldwide evangelization will become a realistic possibility only when the Spirit renews the church in truth and wisdom, faith, holiness, love and power. We therefore call upon all Christians to pray for such a visitation of the sovereign Spirit of God that all his fruit may appear in all his people and that all his gifts may enrich the body of Christ. Only then will the whole church become a fit instrument in his hands, that the whole earth may hear his voice.

(I Cor. 2:4; John 15:26, 27; 16:8–11; I Cor. 12:3; John 3:6–8; II Cor. 3:18; John 7:37–39; I Thess. 5:19; Acts 1:8; Psa. 85:4–7; 67:1–3; Gal. 5:22, 23; I Cor. 12:4–31; Rom. 12:3–8)

15. The Return of Christ

We believe that Jesus Christ will return personally and visibly, in power and glory, to consummate his salvation and his judgment. This promise of his coming is a further spur to our evangelism, for we remember his words that the Gospel must first be preached to all nations. We believe that the interim period between Christ's ascension and return is to be filled with the mission of the people of God, who have no liberty to stop before the End. We also remember his warning that false Christs and false prophets will arise as precursors of the final Antichrist. We therefore reject as a proud, self-confident dream the notion that man can ever build a utopia on earth. Our Christian confidence is that God will perfect his kingdom, and we look forward with eager anticipation to that day, and to the new heaven and earth in which righteousness will dwell and God will reign for ever. Meanwhile, we rededicate ourselves to the service of Christ and of men in joyful submission to his authority over the whole of our lives.

(Mark 14:62; Heb. 9:28; Mark 13:10; Acts 1:8–11; Matt. 28:20; Mark 13:21–23; John 2:18; 4:1–3; Luke 12:32; Rev. 21:1–5; II Pet. 3:13; Matt. 28:18)

Conclusion

Therefore, in the light of this our faith and our resolve, we enter into a solemn covenant with God and with each other, to pray, to plan and to work together for the evangelization of the whole world. We call upon others to join us. May God help us by his grace and for his glory to be faithful to this our covenant! Amen, Alleluia!

(International Congress on World Evangelization, Lausanne, Switzerland, July 1974)
© 1975 World Wide Publications

Appendix 3: 'Evangelical Social Action' The Madras Declaration

1. Preamble

The critical situation of social, economic and political instability prevailing in our country has taken on unprecedented dimensions. The secular nature of our country is being threatened by the increasing oppression of the underprivileged classes, the continuing entrenchment of casteism and the rising rate of communal violence. Politicians devoid of loyalty to truth have precipitated a leadership crisis resulting in a total loss of confidence by the public. The percentage of the population living below the poverty line has risen from forty to sixty in the last six years. The gains of development are mainly benefiting the top ten per cent of our society who control the Indian economy, while masses of people are shackled by abject poverty. Religious leaders and gurus, despite their increasing number and activity, have failed to address themselves to the pressing problems of the masses.

In this context we evangelicals have not been sufficiently compassionate, concerned, or united in our response, mainly because we were uncertain about the biblical basis for social action.

Therefore the Devlali Continuation Committee felt led of the Lord to call a conference to study this matter and to discover ways and means to put into practice whatever the Lord may teach us.

2. Commitment

As Indian evangelicals committed to the Lordship of Christ and to the authority of the Bible, we, the participants of this historic All-India Conference on Evangelical Social Action meeting at Madras from the 2nd to the 5th of October 1979, seek God's help to fulfil the following commitments:

We acknowledge that central to God's nature is His love and justice. God revealed Himself in historical acts of deliverance of His people from slavery, in destroying the unjust kingdoms of Samaria and Judah, and supremely in Jesus, His Son. Jesus' commitment to liberate men from unjust relationships and create right relationships between God and man, and man and man, climaxed in His rejection and death. His resurrection confirms that the cross establishes God's justice and that His return will usher in full and final justice.

We acknowledge that God called out a people to be the community of His kingdom. They are called to model His love and justice in their economic, social and political relationships, and to be instruments of His action in society.

We thank God that social concern has been a partner of evangelism in our land, with a variety of expression and richness of results. We thank God for our evangelical heritage that calls us to listen afresh to the Bible in every new situation.

God's Word Calls Us to Recognise

A. That whereas the scope of God's concern of love and justice, and His historical acts of renewal embrace the whole creation, we have narrowed it only to the rescue of His people from a corrupt world.

185

For this we repent and commit ourselves to a process of education of the Church in the socio-economic and political realities of our land and in her mission.

B. That whereas every man is made in God's image and is the object of His undeserved love, and so has inalienable human dignity and rights which cannot be gifted or removed by any human agency, we have failed in our responsibility to define and defend them.

For this we repent and commit ourselves:

To identify violations of human rights and assist the victims in obtaining their legitimate rights.

To assist the Church in its education programme on human rights.

C. That whereas God calls the Church to model true humanity and prophetically call society to renounce the false gods of mere economic growth at the cost of human rights and progress towards God, we have failed to critically evaluate our involvement in development.

For this we repent and commit ourselves:

To assess critically the role of Christian institutions for education, health, agriculture and relief and any institutions having this allied concern according to the principles of people's participation, justice and service to the poorest.

To assist these institutions to initiate programmes which follow these principles.

D. That whereas the Bible witnesses that God's action included judgement upon systemic evils like poverty and injustice, we have identified the Bible's view of sin only with personal, spiritual, and moral rebellion and wrongdoing.

For this we repent and commit ourselves:

To challenge structures of evil and injustice by speaking up for truth and righteousness and refusing to co-operate with structures and laws which in our opinion promote injustice.

To challenge and correct social sins like dowry, bribery and corruption, especially within the Christian community.

E. That whereas Jesus defined God's mission as the establishment of His kingdom, we have often narrowed the scope of God's kingdom activity to making individuals new creatures and alleviating distress.

For this we repent and commit ourselves:

To assist the community of the King to demonstrate structures of justice.

To be the agent of the kingdom in society to create social structures which preserve and promote human rights and establish peace and dignity.

To encourage evangelicals who have the potential for political leadership to be involved in the work of feeder agencies such as student unions, trade unions and local councils.

To train men of integrity to become leaders who can in turn influence those in legislative and executive bodies.

F. That whereas God's mission in Christ to establish His kingdom included forgiveness of sins and reconciliation with God in the context of social justice, we have failed to see that the scope of God's mission delivers the poor from their destitution, challenges unjust structures and systems and demonstrates new economic, social and political relationships in the life of the community of the King.

For this we repent and commit ourselves:

To encourage local congregations to form appropriate bodies competent to deal with issues related to social action.

G. That whereas Jesus identified injustice and took sides with women and social outcasts of his day, tax collectors, lepers and Samaritans, in our concern to be distinct from the world and its values we have isolated the community of the King from other human communities.

For this we repent and commit ourselves:

To model in our families the Biblical relationships of equality between men and women, employers and servants, rich and poor.
To counteract the communalistic spirit in our land by crossing barriers of wealth, colour, caste and religion.

H. That whereas the simplicity of Jesus' lifestyle was part of His identification with man, we have encouraged personal and corporate lifestyles that have prevented us from identifying with poor and outcaste people.

For this we repent and commit ourselves:

To seriously reduce spending money on non-essentials and thus reduce personal needs to the minimum especially in the areas of food, clothing and housing.
To give faithfully to the Lord and thereby make funds available for the total mission of the Church.

I. That whereas Jesus' own commitment to justice led to suffering and death on the cross, we have often been inactive on issues of justice in the interests of our personal and institutional securities.

For this we repent and commit ourselves:

To return good for evil at all times and thus manifest the Spirit of Christ.

To face martyrdom, if need be, for the defence of the faith and the cause of justice.

f. That whereas the victory of Jesus Christ is expressed in His Lordship over all creation, we have narrowed this to individual victory over sin and His final victory at the second coming. We have lacked the joy and confidence of a people invited to the wedding feast of the King and now feasting at His table.

For this we repent and commit ourselves:

To joyful celebration of His victory in our worship, singing, fellowship and expectations of His victory in the world.

3. *Convictions*

In making these commitments we are convinced that:

WHILE AFFIRMING that the Church is an instrument of God in bringing His justice into society, we cannot accept that social action in itself will liberate individuals and systems from sin.

WHILE AFFIRMING that the Gospel must be preached with relevance to the social context, we cannot accept that social action is the only and entire mission of the Church.

WHILE AFFIRMING that the Church should co-operate without compromise with those working for social change, we cannot accept any other basis for membership of the Church than personal commitment to Jesus as Saviour and Lord.

WHILE AFFIRMING that the Church must be involved in bringing social justice, if necessary by satyagraha and other means of non-violent resistance, we cannot accept that she support, or have partnership in, violent means to achieve this end.

WHILE AFFIRMING that environmental and systemic changes are necessary concerns of the community of the King, we emphatically assert that it is the Lord Jesus alone who through the power of the Holy Spirit frees people from sin that they may glorify God through works of righteousness, thus lending credence to all other changes.

4. *Action*

In view of the actions which we are committing ourselves to we desire to make available to the Church both nationally and locally a servant body who will:

(1) Represent to the government and other authorities the needs of suffering peoples, irrespective of caste, creed, race or sex;

(2) Sponsor seminars and study conferences on issues relating to social action;

(3) Make people aware of the availability of resources at the disposal of the Government and other agencies for purposes of relief and development;

(4) Evaluate measures being taken to fulfil God's demands for righteousness and justice and suggest corrective action, wherever necessary;

(5) Receive complaints from individuals and groups concerning violation of human rights, investigate the same, and, if found true, recommend remedial measures to the parties against whom the complaints have been lodged.

© All India Magazine, Evangelical Fellowship of India, Delhi, November 1979.

Bibliography

Detailed bibliographies are provided for each chapter of the book, referring to the specific topics covered in the various chapters.

Chapter one

Radical discipleship reflects the growing awareness among evangelical Christians that action for social justice is part of the Christian mission. This growing awareness can be traced in the following documents and books:

Let the Earth Hear His Voice edited by J. D. Douglas (World Wide Publications 1975) reproduces the papers, responses and resolutions of the Lausanne Congress. Of special interest are the papers by René Padilla and Samuel Escobar, and the statement on Radical Discipleship. John Stott produced a *Commentary on the Lausanne Covenant*, Lausanne Occasional Papers No 3. His book *Mission in the Modern World* (Falcon 1975) gave a post-Lausanne look at the relation between evangelism and social action. Ron Sider in *Evangelism Salvation and Social Justice* (Grove Booklets on Ethics No 16 1977) takes up the debate from Lausanne and allows John Stott a last word in the appendix.

The Lausanne Congress was followed up in a number of ways. A series of world wide study groups were initiated by the Lausanne

Committee and the World Evangelical Fellowship to study the meaning of the Covenant's commitment to Simple Lifestyle. The papers of the concluding consultation and the 'Evangelical Commitment to Simple Lifestyle' are published in *Lifestyle in the 80's: An Evangelical Commitment to Simple Lifestyle* edited by R. J. Sider (Paternoster 1981).

The major follow up to Lausanne was the Consultation on World Evangelisation at Thailand in 1980. Of the reports from that consultation now being published, the reports which show the concerns of Radical Discipleship most clearly are *Christian Witness to the Urban Poor* and *Christian Witness to Marxists*, Lausanne Occasional Papers forthcoming.

On a world level, *The New Face of Evangelicalism* edited by René Padilla (Hodder and Stoughton 1975) examines the biblical basis for the concern of the Lausanne Congress for a whole gospel for the whole world. In India, the Devlali Congress on Mission and Evangelism took up the themes of Lausanne in an Indian context and published the findings in *Go Forth and Tell* (Evangelical Fellowship of India 1977). The Devlali Congress sponsored a further study conference on evangelical social action in 1979 which produced *The Madras Declaration on Evangelical Social Action* which is reproduced as an appendix to this book.

In the context of the Church of England, the three books *Obeying Christ in a Changing World* (Collins, Fount 1977) take something of the concerns of Lausanne into the National Evangelical Anglican Congress at Nottingham in 1977. *The Nottingham Statement* (Falcon 1977) and *Evangelicals Tomorrow* by John Capon (Collins Fount 1977) present the discussions and findings of the congress.

David Lyon in *Christians and Sociology* (IVP 1975) draws some of the teeth of the charges that sociology undermines faith. J. A. Walter in *A Long Way from Home* (Paternoster 1979) gives a penetrating insight into the myths of western society and seeks to develop a Christian sociological perspective based on the fall. David Sheppard in *Built as a City* (Hodder and Stoughton 1974) poses hard questions to a church that would ignore the sociology of cities. Why is it that people who become Christians in the inner city get up and leave – and why are more Christians found among groups that have the best houses, education, environment and working conditions?

Jose Miguez Bonino in *Christians and Marxists* (Hodder and Stoughton 1976) sees this as a world wide phenomenon of a gospel permeated with cultural values rather than biblical ones. Michael Eastman and others in *Inside Out* (Falcon 1976) draw on experience of youth work to show the place of social systems and social forces on young lives. Ron Sider in *Rich Christians in an age of hunger* (Hodder and Stoughton 1978) and Susan George in *How the Other Half Dies* (Pelican 1977) move to the broader canvas of the systems of world trade that produce poverty.

A useful set of booklets on poverty and development in India is produced by the Centre for Social Action, 64 Millers Road, Bangalore 46. *The Indian Situation* by Duarte Barreto forms part of this series. Robert Holman's book *Poverty: Explanations of Social Deprivation* (Martin Robertson 1979) gives a helpful survey of the analyses of poverty and powerlessness in Britain. His understanding of the causes of poverty is very helpful for appreciating the situation in India too.

The movement for renewal in the Spirit is documented in books by Michael Harper and Graham Pulkingham published by Hodder and Stoughton. Michael Harper brings many lessons for the life of the local church together in *Let My People Grow* (Hodder and Stoughton 1977).

The questions for interpreting the Bible posed by Liberation Theology can be found in Jose Miguez Bonino *Christians and Marxists* (Hodder and Stoughton 1976), Gustavo Guttierez *Theology of Liberation* (SCM 1977), Jose Porfirio Miranda *Marx and the Bible* (SCM 1977) and Andrew Kirk *Liberation Theology: An Evangelical View from the Third World* (Marshall Morgan and Scott 1979). For further books see the bibliography to chapter 17.

David Watson in *I Believe in Evangelism* (Hodder and Stoughton 1976) and *I Believe in the Church* (Hodder and Stoughton 1978) explores the lifestyle and communication methods of St Michael-le-Belfry Church, York. The biblical basis of the church as redeemed persons in community is developed by David Watson in *I Believe in the Church* and John Stott in *God's New Society: The message of Ephesians* (IVP 1979).

Chapter two

Ron Sider's *Rich Christians in an Age of Hunger* (Hodder, 1978) gives examples of sharing resources and a bibliography. The Shaftesbury Project Overseas Aid group who edited the British edition have also provided a directory of organisations concerned with issues of justice and development and noted the games, literature and other resources they offer. F. C. Schumacher's *Small is*

Beautiful (Abacus, 1973) and John V. Taylor's *Enough is Enough* (SCM, 1975) have become two classics in the simple lifestyle literature, combining argument with examples. More recently, John White has examined the problem of materialism, the other side of the lifestyle issue, in *The Golden Cow* (Marshall Morgan and Scott, 1979), and Richard J. Foster contributes a chapter of his book on spirituality *Celebration of Discipline* (Hodder, 1980) to the biblical grounding of simple living as part of Christian spirituality.

David Clark surveys one hundred and five Christian-inspired communities in *Basic Communities* (SPCK, 1977). He defines community as a feeling of solidarity and significance which people have about each other. These are 'basic' groups because they form a base where people can live and work while attempting to 'return to the roots of being human'. Charles Mellis in *Committed Communities – Fresh Streams of World Mission* (William Carey Library, 1976) traces the inner-core committed groups as a vanguard of Christian mission throughout Church history in the monastic movement, anabaptist groups, and nineteenth century missionary societies. He assesses its positive role today in areas of mission. Derek Tidball gives a cautious survey of Christian community living in 'The New Gospel of Community', *Third Way*, April 1980.

Occasional but vitally important literature from many groups wrestling with the problems of Christian social involvement 'up-front' does not find its way into libraries, bookshops or even church bookstalls. But it is in this literature that key thoughts and experiments are shared. There is the long running newsletter of '*Christians in Industrial Areas*' available from Mrs Sheila Turner, St Gabriel's Vicarage, Seel Road, Huyton Quarry, Liverpool L36 6DT.

The *Latin American Theological Fraternity* publishes monographs on evangelical theology of liberation, with some of the best writing of René Padilla and Samuel Escobar who gave the lead to the radical discipleship movement at the Lausanne Congress in 1974 available in their series. The Bulletin of the LATF is available from Ave. Plutarco E Calles No 1962, Col. Prado, Mexico 13 – D.F. *Shaft* is the newsletter of the Shaftesbury Project and carries reports of study-groups of the project. It is available from 8 Oxford Street, Nottingham. *Frontier* develops theology and reflection on Christian youth work, and is sent out by the *Frontier Youth Trust*, 130 City Road, London EC1V 2NJ. FYT also publish a very useful resource manual, *Source and Resources*. Sojourners, a biblical magazine with regular articles on economic justice, discipleship and community is published from 1029 Vermont Avenue, NW, Washington D.C. 20005. A magazine with similar concerns, but perhaps more of a sense of humour is *The Other Side*, Box 12236 Philadelphia PA 19144. In the UK, *Third Way Magazine*, 130 City Road, London EC1 is building an understanding of discipleship in the full economic, social, political and global context of our world. In Australia, *On Being* magazine focuses on the same themes and is available from 2 Denham Street, Hawthorn 3122, Australia. In the Philippines, The Institute for the Study of Asian Church and Culture (ISACC) produces *Patmos* which they describe as a 'forum seeking a joyous and an authentic Asian witness to Christ and His Kingdom'. It is available from ISACC, 12-B Sorsogon Street, West Avenue, Quezon City, P.O. Box 481, Greenhill, Metro Manila, Philippines.

David Sheppard distils his experience from over ten years as warden of the Mayflower Centre in Canning Town, London in *Built as a City* (Hodder, 1974). Roger Sainsbury draws on experience in Shrewsbury House, Everton in *Inside Out* edited by Michael Eastman (Falcon, 1976), and in *From a Mersey Wall* (Scripture Union). Julian Charley, the present warden of Shrewsbury House brings the story up to date in 'Goodness and Mersey', *Third Way* No. 7, April 1977. Roger Dowley writes of his experience of Inner City Living and its pro's and con's in *Shaft*, the Shaftesbury Project Newsletter, June 1977. The Shaftesbury Project Inner City group published a study paper in 1980 entitled *'Powerlessness and the Inner City – Some Reflections'*. The paper understands inner city problems as an example of wider factors of power and powerlessness in society, discusses biblical material and gives practical examples of inner city groups organising themselves to resist what they perceive as unfair treatment.

One of the leading Christian economists in India is C. T. Kurien. His major works are *Poverty and Development* (Christian Literature Service, Park Town, Madras, India, 1974) and *Poverty, Planning and Social Transformation* (Allied Publishers, 13/14 Asaf Ali Road, New Delhi 110002). Francois Houtart gives a survey of relief and development projects of the Catholic Church in India in *The Development Projects as a Social Practice of the Catholic Church in India* (Louvain, 1976). He concludes that very few out of over 6000 projects do anything significant to tackle the real socio-political and cultural causes of poverty. Gunnar Myrdal's classic *Asian Drama* (abridged version, Pelican, 1978) and David Selbourne *An Eye to India* (Pelican, 1977) give further documentation on the situation in India.

Literature from the Renewal Movement is vast. Michael Green's *I Believe in the Holy Spirit* (Hodder, 1974) gives a sympathetic theological perspective. Howard Snyder in *New Wine New Wineskins* (Marshall, Morgan and Scott, 1977) raises some of the questions for the structures of Christian fellowship. Arnold Bittlinger reviews the implications for ministry in *Gifts and Ministries* (Hodder and Stoughton, 1974) and in *Gifts and Graces* (Hodder and Stoughton). Michael Green draws water from many streams in his paper 'Mission and Ministry' in *The People of God*, Volume II of *Obeying Christ in a Changing World* edited by Ian Cundy in the series edited by John Stott (Found, 1977). He develops every-member team-led ministry for today's church. Michael Harper's *Let My People Grow* (Hodder, 1977) is the magnum opus on the Holy Spirit and ministry in the church. The positive way in which the movement for renewal in the Holy Spirit is also concerned for issues of social justice is reflected in the publication *Towards Renewal*, from the Post Green Community, 57 Dorchester Road, Lytchett Minster, Poole, Dorset, BH16 6JE.

The concern of the Lausanne Covenant to develop a simple lifestyle in order to contribute more generously to both relief and evangelism (article 9), was followed up by a number of consultations on Simple Lifestyle around the world. The documents of the United States Consultation on Simple Lifestyle are reproduced in *Living More Simply: Biblical Principles and Practical Models* edited by Ronald Sider (IVP, USA, 1980 and Hodder and Stoughton, 1980). These consultations culminated in the International Consultation on Simple Lifestyle in London, March 1980, sponsored by the Lausanne Committee for World Evangelisation and the World Evangelical Fellowship Theological Commission Unit on Ethics and Society. The papers from this are published in *Lifestyle in the 80's: An Evangelical Commitment to Simple Lifestyle* edited by R. J. Sider (Paternoster, 1981). The W.E.F. Theological Commission Unit on Ethics and Society also sponsored a consultation on Theology of Development in March 1980. The papers are published in *Evangelicals and Development: Towards a Theology of Social Change* edited by R. J. Sider (Paternoster, 1981).

I am indebted to Aslancrafts Education Unit for information that recently evangelical house church groups have begun to focus on social issues. A group centred in Bradford produces a magazine called 'Restoration', with a circulation of 11,000, and supports a worker in appropriate technology in Africa. A group in Middlesbrough, Middlesbrough Centre Piece, runs a coffee shop, a craft centre selling Third World crafts, and a reconditioning centre for essential tools for carpenters etc. to send overseas.

Traidcraft, an evangelical trading concern for Third World goods, is also developing a project for unemployed youth in its Newcastle centre.

Michael Eastman of the Frontier Youth Trust, with an eye to the British scene, reports that issues of social justice were raised at the Scripture Union International Council Meetings in 1979, published in *Share the Word* (Ark Publishing, 1979) at the Nationwide Initiative in Evangelism Assembly in 1980, and in the National Pastoral Congress of the Roman Catholic Church. An Evangelical Coalition for Urban Mission is being formed at the time of writing incorporating the Frontier Youth Trust, the Evangelical Race Relations Group, the Evangelical Urban Training Project, the 'Christians in Industrial Areas' Correspondence and the Shaftesbury Project.

Chapter three

A full defence of every statement in this chapter would require a library of theological books. Practically everything in the Gospels has been questioned at some time or other. There are also, among evangelicals, many debates on the significance of Jesus' ministry to Israel and the meaning of his ministry to 'the poor'.

I have attempted to state some of the emphases in Jesus' ministry, especially his politics and concern for the poor, which the radical discipleship movement stresses. A significant text is John Yoder, *The politics of Jesus* (Eerdmans, 1972). It is debated by Anthony Thistleton and Michael Garde in *Shaft*, the Shaftesbury Project journal, September 1977. In *The original revolution* (Herlad Press, 1971), Yoder deals with the relationship between Jesus, the kingdom and the Church. George Eldon Ladd in *A theology of the New Testament* (Lutterworth, 1975) and *I believe in the resurrection* (Hodder, 1975), draws out the eschatological thrust of New Testament theology and is especially commended to those who doubt that Paul had the same eschatological interests as Jesus. Victor Paul Furnish in *The love command in the New Testament* (SCM, 1973) and *Theology and ethics in Paul* (Abingdon, 1968) develops this further. Stephen Travis gives an excellent introduction to

195

eschatology in *The Jesus hope* (Word, 1975), and in *Christian hope and the future of man* (IVP, 1980).

C. H. Dodd gives a gem-like study of Jesus' ministry in *The founder of Christianity* (Collins, 1971). John Desrochers gives a study of Jesus' ministry with questions of justice in mind in *Christ the liberator* (Centre for Social Action, 64 Millers Road, Benson Town, Bangalore 560046, India, n.d.). In *Jesus, politics and society* (Orbis, 1978), Richard J. Cassidy discusses in detail the material in Luke's Gospel bearing on Jesus' political involvement. His thesis can be summarised by the following, from p. 59:

> Jesus is not at all intimidated by a particular social order, or by the rulers who hold high offices within it. He does not hestitate to advocate substantially different social patterns, and he does not defer to the established rulers or hestitate to criticise them.

Tom Wright and Michael Sadgrove point out the theology of Jesus' ministry in 'Jesus Christ the only Saviour', in *Obeying Christ in a Changing World: 1, The Lord Christ* edited by John Stott (Collins Fountain, 1977). Martin Hengel, *Victory over violence* (Philadelphia, 1973), discusses Jesus and the political parties.

For the social, economic and political implications of Jesus' ministry, see Vinay Samuel, *The meaning and cost of discipleship*, published by BUILD, 11 Sujata Co-op Housing Society, SV Road, Bandra, Bombay 400050 (1981). I am indebted to discussions with Vinay during his preparation of these Bishop Joshi memorial lectures, for his insights into Jesus' interpretation of the Jewish law – developed in the book. John Goldingay's lecture, 'Exodus and liberation', *Tyndale Bulletin*, 1976, is a rich resource for the biblical concept of liberation.

The author has discussed some of these issues of Jesus' ministry in:

Social gospel or no gospel (Grove Booklets on Ethics 4, 1975)

A different dream (Grove Booklets on Ethics 12, 1976)

'The kingdom and the kingdoms', *Third Way* 1(13), June 1977 and 2(14) July 1977.

Jesus the Liberator, a programmed learning course for Extension Education, TAFTEE, P O Box 520, Cooke Town, Bangalore 560005, India. The author discusses this course in 'Teaching Christ as liberator in extension education' in *Evangelical review of theology* (Pasternoster Press), 4(1), April 1980.

An important area of research is the extent to which John's Gospel echoes Luke's portrait of Jesus' involvement with the poor and outcast. Jose Porfirio Miranda's study *Being and the Messiah – the message of John* (Orbis, 1977) provides helpful material.

For Jesus' ministry to the poor, Ron Sider's *Rich Christians . . .*, already mentioned, delves exhaustively into the biblical material. Sider casts a wider net in *Cry Justice* (Paulist Press, 1980). Jim Wallis has a helpful section on the Church, the poor and the powerless in *Agenda for biblical people* (Harper, 1976). Julio de Santaana surveys the biblical material and the Church's economic practice historically, in *Good news for the poor* (Christian Literature Service, Madras, 1978; and WCC, 1978). Martin Hengel, *Property and riches in the early church* (SCM, 1977) covers similar ground. Peter Davis examines the Gospel evidence in '*The poor man's gospel*', Themelios, Summer 1976. The study at the Consultation on World Evangelisation in 1980 on *Christian witness to the urban poor* includes a major study on biblical words for the poor. It is to be published by the Lausanne Committee for World Evangelisation in 1981–2. Recent studies also include *Rich man, poor man and the Bible* by Conrad Boerma (SCM, 1979) and David L. Mealand's *Poverty and expectation in the Gospels* (SPCK, 1980).

Chapter four

'On Easter morning there dawned the last day of history. The New Age is here; history as we know it is in process of being wound up: the Creator has finished the first and chief task of his new creation, and thus has laid the foundation of the completion of the rest.' Michael Sadgrove and Tom Wright superbly summarise the biblical theology of salvation in 'Jesus Christ the only Saviour' in *Obeying Christ in a changing world. 1. The Lord Christ* (Collins Fountain, 1977) by focusing on the whole nexus of Jesus' life, death, resurrection, Spirit and return. George Eldon Ladd writes excellently on the meaning of the Resurrection in *I believe in the Resurrection* (Hodder, 1975).

On social sin, David Moberg gives a profound analysis of the shallowness of much Christian thinking in *The great reversal* (Scripture Union, 1973): Ron Sider in *Rich Christians in an age of hunger* (IVP, 1977) goes through the biblical material on solidarity and responsibility: Jim Wallis in *Agenda for biblical people* (Harper, 1976) and John Yoder in *The politics of Jesus* (Eerdmans, 1972) outline a theology of the powers. Ron Sider and John Stott discuss this further in *Evangelism, salvation and social justice* (Grove Booklets on Ethics 16, 1976) and George Carey in 'Falling structures

– a discussion of the meaning of structural sin', *Third Way*, 8 September 1977, writes helpfully on understanding social sin in our present context.

Material on Jesus' resistance to evil and Christian suffering, can be found in John Yoder's *Politics of Jesus* (*op. cit.*), the writings of Martin Luther King, especially *Strength to Love* (Fontana, 1974), and in Harvey Seifert *Conquest through Suffering* (Westminster, 1965).

Chapter five

Howard Snyder presents seminal thinking on the church in *New wine, new wineskins* (Marshall Morgan and Scott, 1977), developing his paper given at the Lausanne congress. Jim Wallis in *Agenda for biblical people* (Harper, 1976) represents similar thinking in stressing the function of the church as the community of the kingdom.

Since this thinking brings the visible church into the centre of evangelical discussion, I have also drawn on Ian Cundy's paper for the National Evangelical Anglican Congress 'The Church as Community' in *Obeying Christ in a changing world. 2. The people of God* (Collins Fountain, 1977). Cundy develops some of the implications of Snyder's thinking for the local and universal visible church. Other essays in this volume hammer out some of the difficult structural problems of unity, patterns of ministry and institutionalism.

Michael Harper presents a superb discussion of structures of membership, ministry and leadership in the Church in *Let my people grow* (Hodder, 1977). It is scholarly, biblical and exceedingly down to earth.

Charles Mellis discusses the relationship between committed action groups and wider, more apathetic church groups with particular reference to the growth of voluntary societies like the CMS in the Church of England, in *Committed Communities* (William Carey Library, 1976). Groups which espouse a radical lifestyle or deeper commitment will have to work through their relationship to the wider visible church. The CMS example is a good one to follow.

Chapter six

Two trenchant works criticising the involvement of Christians in society have recently been published. Arthur Johnston, in *The battle for world evangelism* (Tyndale House, 1978), fears that the concerns of the Lausanne Congress will castrate the evangelistic task of the Church, just as the missionary task of the Church was hindered in the first half of the twentieth century because of liberal views of Scripture. The issue here is actually not evangelism, but the content of the gospel; is God's kingdom restricted to right relationships with God, or does it include the whole created order of social relationships and man's physical environment?

Exactly the same issue is raised by a critic of more liberal Christian involvement in politics, E. R. Norman in his BBC Reith lectures *Christianity and world order* (Oxford University Press, 1979). Haddon Willmer and others reply in *Christian faith and political hopes* (Epworth, 1979). Norman concentrates all his attention on what cannot be achieved in the social sphere because of the fall of man. Willmer and his colleagues point out that the pivot of Christianity in the world is not the fall, but redemption. This redemption is restricted by Norman to man's relationship with God; Willmer and his colleagues emphasise that creation and resurrection give a hope for redeeming man's social relationships and the physical order now. The lectures are also well discussed by Andrew Kirk, 'Edward Norman and political involvement', *Third Way*, January 1980.

Christianity and social order by William Temple (Penguin, 1942) covers much ground now being rediscovered by Christians, and discovered for the first time by evangelicals. It contains a solid criticism of laissez-faire capitalism, arguing from a theology of creation, and sets out many arguments for a Welfare State. He also discusses the role of the Church as the Church in politics. H. F. R. Catherwood in *The Christian in industrial society* (Tyndale Press, 1964), *The Christian citizen* (Hodder, 1978), and *A better way* (IVP, 1975), makes an important case for the involvement of individual Christians in society. But he does not go nearly far enough in applying the gospel to society. Orlando E. Costas in *The Church and its mission, a shattering critique from the Third World* (Tyndale House, 1974) has a far more satisfactory theology of Church and society and analyses the strength and weakness of concentrating on Church growth to the exclusion of issues of discipleship in society.

For a discussion of the relationship between Israelite society and land tenure, see Christopher Wright, *What does the Lord require?* (Shaftesbury Project, 1979), and Vinay Samuel and Chris Sugden, 'A just and responsible lifestyle' (paper presented at the

International Consultation on Simple Lifestyle, March 1980, at present unpublished).

Since this book was completed, two important contributions to evangelical Christians' social thinking have appeared: *God's people in God's world* by John Gladwin (IVP, 1979), and Alan Storkey's *A Christian social perspective* (IVP, 1979).

Chapter seven

The Way, by Geoffrey Robinson and Stephen Winward was first published by Scripture Union in 1945, and revised in 1961. John Pollock's biography of *William Wilberforce* was published by Lion Publishing, 1977.

Vinay Samuel's *The meaning and cost of discipleship* examines in detail the context and meaning of Jesus' call to discipleship (see bibliography to chapter 3 for details).

I am indebted to Athol Gill's unpublished lectures on *The call to discipleship*, for its pointing out of the significance of Jesus' invitation to people to follow him.

Chapter nine

The following materials give an insight into the issues of poverty and development in India.

Poverty and Development – A programmed course for individual and group study, published by The Association for Theological Extension Education, P.O. Box 520, Bangalore 560005, India, and SEARCH, 256 Off 7th Cross, Jayanagar 1 Block, Bangalore 560011, India, written by John Staley and Chris Sugden. *Affluence, Poverty and the Word of God* by Klaus Nurnberger, Lutheran Publishing House, Durban, 1978, outlines the economic and ideological issues and strategies to which the biblical material on the poor is relevant. An excellent introduction to the Bible and economics is found in J. Philip Wogaman *The Great Economic Debate – An Ethical Analysis* (SCM, 1977). Donald Hay also provides important material in *A Christian Critique of Capitalism* (Grove Books, 1975). All three books look at the ideologies and strategies of economic systems in the light of the Bible.

A fine survey of the many ways in which a relief and development agency is involved round the world is Alf MaCreay's *Up with people: Christian Aid around the world* (Collins Fount, 1979).

With his colleague, Vinay Samuel, the author has jointly written '*An overview of the literature on theology of development*' published in *Evangelicals and Development: Towards a theology of social change* edited by R. J. Sider (Paternoster, 1981).

A comprehensive resource guide for materials on development issues for use by groups is available in *The Development Puzzle* published by VCOAD, Parnell House, Wilton Road, London SW1. *Aslancrafts Education Unit*, 86 Potternewton Lane, Leeds 7, are an evangelical Christian group producing resources for church groups. Their pack, *Education for Justice* contains materials for groups to use in four meetings, and introduces issues of injustice internationally, within Third World countries and within the United Kingdom. It includes biblical material on justice, simulation games, guides for group discussion, resources for prayer and worship, and suggestions for group action. *Christians for Justice in Development*, 13 Osterley Park Road, Southall, Middlesex, are a similar evangelical group committed to stimulating outspoken Christian witness for social justice in which faith in Christ is central. Ron Sider's *Rich Christians in an age of hunger* (Hodder, 1978) contains a bibliography and a directory of British organisations committed to working for development and justice. One of these, the *World Development Movement*, 26 Bedford Chambers, Covent Garden, London WC2, is a secular organisation for development and justice which many Christian groups are finding a useful source of material and a useful channel for taking part in work for justice in development. The *Shaftesbury Project*, 8 Oxford Street, Nottingham, is publishing a handbook of world needs which introduces biblical material and practical guides for Christians to be effectively involved in world development and social justice.

Waldron Scott, the former general secretary of the World Evangelical Fellowship, has contributed a study on the mission of the church and social justice in *Bring Forth Justice* (Eerdmans, 1980). He takes the issues of poverty and injustice, and God's concern for social justice into the area of the work of establishment evangelical missionary societies, the training of missionary candidates and the basic process of discipleship training. He writes: 'There is a need to study the Bible through the eyes of the poor: develop solid biblically based convictions related to discipleship and global justice; make firm and joint commitments to the service of the poor; reorient lifestyle, evangelism, disciplemaking and service to reflect identification with the poor; and become involved in their struggle.' (p. 248).

Dr Tom Sine, of the evangelical relief and development agency

World Concern, based in Seattle, USA, is producing a book entitled *The Mustard Seed Conspiracy, Making a World of Difference in a World of Need* (Word Books forthcoming). He gathers examples where insignificant groups and projects are showing concern for all the right relationships of the kingdom as they share its good news.

Jorgen Lissner has documented the thesis that relief and development agencies tend to avoid the consequences of a stance for justice because of their need to raise support in *The Politics of Altruism* (Lutheran World Federation, 1978).

Chapter eleven

David Watson's *I believe in evangelism* (Hodder, 1976) is a recent classic on the subject, but as one reviewer perceptively commented, it only deals with evangelism among middle-class people in England.

Inside Out (ed. Michael Eastman) (Falcon, 1976) is a stimulating selection of essays on evangelism among young people, particularly in inner cities. *Third Way Magazine* ran a series of articles to explore the convergence and divergence concerning evangelism which could be discerned between the Lausanne Covenant, the statement from the WCC Nairobi Congress, and the papal exhortation 'Evangelii Nuntiandi'. These articles together with responses are in the issues Vol I No 23, 1 December 1977 to Vol 2 No 4, 23 February 1978. They are entitled:

'World Evangelisation', John Stott (1 December 1977)
'Replies to John Stott' by Gerald Bray, Herbert Carson, Roger Forster and Leith Samuel (15 December 1977)
'Different Worlds', Bishop David Brown (12 January 1978)
'The Slow Road to Convergence', John Richardson (26 January 1978)
'Evangelistic Synthesis', Robert Bogan (9 February 1978)
'Springs Need No Pumps', Morgan Derham (23 February 1978).

Chapter twelve

René Padilla writes piercingly and pungently on repentance in 'Evangelism and the world' in the report of the Lausanne Conference on World Evangelisation: J. D. Douglas (ed.), *Let the earth hear his voice* (World-wide Publications, 1975), pp. 116–133.

Chapter thirteen

Michael Harper's essay 'Christian maturity' in *Obeying Christ in a changing world: 1, the Lord Christ* (ed. John Stott) (Collins Fountain, 1977) gathers wisdom from wide experience in pastoral care. *The Nottingham statement* (Falcon, 1977), produced by the second National Evangelical Anglican Congress has a section on Christian maturing that condenses much into a small space. Kevin Shergold in 'Suburban realities', in: Michael Eastmann (ed.), *Inside out* (Falcon, 1976), p. 26–40, writes very helpfully on helping young people develop a Christian life of their own. Howard Snyder in *New wine, new wineskins* (Marshall Morgan & Scott, 1977) discusses the necessity for small groups for Christians' growth, reminding us of John Wesley's example in his chapters 11 and 15.

Chapter fourteen

Peter Lee's *Equipping God's people: Present and Future Parish Training Schemes* (Grove Booklets on Ministry and Worship No. 45, 1976) lists and comments on many new initiatives in training. A very impressive syllabus is offered at The Jesus Centre, Birmingham.

Basic Christian Teaching (headings only are given here)

1 The Gospel
2 The Church
3 The Normal Christian
4 The Work of the Spirit
5 Practical Evangelism
6 The Christian Community
7 The History of the Church
8 What Shall I Do?
9 Healing
10 Spiritual Warfare
11 Prayer
12 Ministries in the Church
13 An Introduction to the Bible
14 Relationships
15 Meditation Series
16 Expositions of Books of the Bible

Social Questions

1. THE CHRISTIAN ATTITUDE TO: Pornography – Abortion – Homosexuality – Vandalism – War – Demonstrations – Censorship.
2. CHRISTIANITY AND. . . . Science – Economics – Politics – Race Relations – Trades Unions – Business Management – The Press – Radio and TV.

3. How a city is organised: The Council – Power Structures – Housing – Roads – Youth – Old People – Education – The Arts – Health and Medicine – Commerce – Social Services.
4. The Christian church overseas: In North America – In Europe – In the Warsaw Pact countries – In the Middle East – In South America – In Africa – In India – In S.E. Asia – In China.
5. International problems: The pollution problem – The population problem – The economic problem.
6. Psychology and Christianity: Understanding myself – Depression – Fear – Anxiety – Recognising mental illness – Counselling others – Guilt – Loneliness – Boredom.
7. What they believe: Introduction to Jehovah's Witnesses – Mormons – Christian Science – Christadelphians – 7th Day Adventists – Marxism – Humanism – Freemasonry – Jews – Hindus – Muslims – Sikhs – Buddhists – Shintoists – Animists – Hare Krishna – Divine Light Mission – Scientology – Unified Family – Children of God.
8. Christianity and the arts: Music – Drama – Poetry

Relationships Analysis (Part of hand-out material provided)

Requirements in relationships (Roles)	Acceptance/ Status Protection Love Encouragement Freedom	Forgiveness Sharing/Trust Honesty Explanations Growth Companionship
Difficulties in relationships	– What is expected of those involved in the relationship?	
(Role uncertainty)		
(Role perversion)	Unacceptance Discouragement Restrictiveness Unforgiveness	Mistrust/Fear Dishonesty
Answers to difficulties	(1)	Establishing what each person is wanting out of the relationship.
	(2)	Acknowledge the situation as it exists.
	(3)	Determine the agreed potential for the relationship.
	(4)	Act on it!

QUOTE!! 'I am not in this world to live up to your expectations,
          and you are not in this world to live up to my
          expectations; I am I, and you are you, and when we
          meet it's beautiful.'

Chapter fifteen

Anthony Thiselton describes the necessity and method of interpreting the biblical text in its own context and interpreting it
correctly in today's context, in 'Understanding God's Word today', in *Obeying Christ in a changing world: 1, The Lord Christ* (ed.
John Stott) (Collins Fountain, 1977), p. 90. His magnum opus is
The two horizons (Paternoster Press, 1980).

Bruce Kaye introduces the inductive method of studying the
Bible in his introduction to volume 3 of *Obeying Christ in a
changing world: The changing world* (ed. Bruce Kaye) (Collins
Fountain, 1977), p. 9–16.

For a summary of some of the issues of contextualisation, or
interpreting in context, see: 'The contextualisation debate', in
Gospel in context, July 1979. This journal devoted an entire issue
to a symposium on the subject. It is available from Partnership in
Mission, 1564 Edgehill Road, Abington, Pa. 19001 USA. Ross
Kinsler in 'Mission and context: the current debate about contex-
tualisation' in *Evangelical Missions Quarterly*, 14(1), January 1978,
and Harvey Conn, 'Contextualisation: where do we begin?' in Carl
E. Armeding (ed.), *Evangelicals and Liberation* (Presbyterian and
Reformed Publishing Co., 1977) give helpful surveys of the issues.
Charles Kraft in *Christianity in culture* (Orbis, 1979), and James
Engel in *Contemporary Christian communications* (Nelson, 1979),
discuss the part that culture plays in biblical interpretation and
communication. Andrew Kirk introduced the contribution made
to the debate by Liberation Theology in *Liberation theology: an
evangelical view from the Third World* (Marshall Morgan & Scott,
1979), as does Stephen Knapp in 'A preliminary dialogue with
Gutierrez' *A theology of liberation*' in *Evangelicals and liberation*,
op. cit. The Willowbank Report of the Consultation of the Lausanne Committee Theology and Education Group, *Gospel in culture*, is published as Lausanne Occasional Paper No. 2, 1978
(Scripture Union, 1978), and was summarised in *Third Way*, 1
June 1978. Michael Eastmann introduces some of these concerns
in his article on liberation theology in *Share the Word* (Scripture
Union, 1979).

A prominent exponent of the traditional evangelical deductive method of biblical interpretation is Carl F. Henry, in his five-volume work *God, revelation and authority* (5 vols., Word Books, Texas). We read Scripture, Henry says, to deduce propositional truths from revealed first principles. Two comments from scholars will show the difference between this traditional method and the insights offered by radical discipleship.

Arvind Vos in the *Reformed Journal*, December 1977, suggests that the deductive method is more appropriate for reading a systematic text, like Euclid's *Elements*. 'The Gospels, like the rest of the biblical canon, are in the common sense rather than the systematic mode of presentation. The problem of interpretation arises because common sense is common only to members of a community, and not to all times and places. Every place, city, nation and age has its own brand of common sense.' The difference in the task of interpretation is shown by the fact that there is little exegetical literature on Euclid, but an endless number of commentaries have been written on the Gospels.

John Yoder, in many ways the herald of radical discipleship, speaks from the Mennonite tradition, and discusses Carl Henry's view of Jesus as the Ideal of Christian Ethics in *The Politics of Jesus* (Eerdmans, 1972), p. 131. He writes in footnote 32, 'The description of Jesus is strikingly selective. It centres on motivational virtues (unselfishness, compassion, resisting temptation, meekness, obedience) rather than on ethical specifics. There is no reference to the specific temptation of the Zealot option, and it is expressly denied that Jesus' poverty or celibacy might have any exemplary value . . . Henry . . . represents the tradition that has been able to appropriate much of the New Testament idiom, without catching its central historical thrust.'

Chapter sixteen

Material in this and the previous chapter has been developed from two as yet unpublished papers presented at international conferences, and co-written by Vinay Samuel and the author: *A Third World guide to current trends in theology* (Scripture Union International Council, Madras, 1980) and *Contextualisation and the Christian communicator* (First conference of the Asian Christian Communicator's Fellowship, Taiwan, 1980).

Chapter seventeen

Action represents a commitment. We must be conscious of, and evaluate, what commitments we have. Do they adequately reflect the good news of the Scripture? This is a new question for theology to ask. It represents a new way of doing theology. It does not weaken the place of the Bible in theology; it requires that, rather than merely reading the Bible and coming up with good intentions to act, we reflect on what, in the light of the Bible, our action should be.

We can learn much from the central thesis of liberation theology. It speaks of the liberation of theology, from endless arguments about minute details of doctrine and contemplation of its own navel without active relationship to how people actually live their lives. There are many grounds for criticising liberation theology (see for example, 'One law for the rich?', *Third Way*, October 1978). But I include a summary of important writings which illuminate its concerns. A Latin American, José Miguez Bonino, gives the clearest exposition in *Revolutionary theology comes of age* (SPCK, 1975). Andrew Kirk writes from twelve years' experience in Latin America, in dialogue with liberation theologians, in *Theology encounters revolution* (IVP, 1979). Orlando Costas gives a Latin American evangelical critique of Western theology of mission and liberation theology in *The Church and the mission – A shattering critique from the Third World* (Tyndale House, Illinois, 1974).

Derek Winter describes a journey through Latin America meeting liberation theologians and encountering the situations which prompt them to seek action which represents a Christian commitment to the poor, in *Hope in captivity* (Epworth, 1977). Commitment to the poor prompts liberation theologians to ask serious questions about who produces what and who gets the results. They find Marxist answers most relevant. José Miguez Bonino discusses this in *Christians and Marxists* (Hodder and Stoughton, 1976). For a positive critical assessment of Marx see David Lyon, *Karl Marx: Christian appreciation of his life and thought* (Lion and IVP, 1979). José Porfirio Miranda carefully studies biblical themes of justice and oppression in the light of Marx's questions in *Marx and the Bible* (SCM, 1977). Gustavo Guttiérez, a representative figure of liberation theology, gives a broad survey in *Theology of liberation* (SCM, 1974). Sebastian Kappen discusses liberation theology in an Indian context in *Jesus and freedom* (Orbis, 1977) and adds the important dimension of the need for a parallel inner liberation from selfishness and hate. The author has discussed the appeal of Marxism in Latin America in the forthcoming symposium edited by Patrick Soohkdeo and published by Paternoster Press. A comprehensive introduction to Marxism can be found in David Lyon's *Karl Marx: A Christian appreciation of his life and thought* (Lion and IVP, 1979).

Scan was a bi-monthly survey of publications in the field of Christian mission and social witness. In Spring 1978 it gave a comprehensive survey of literature on Christian dialogue with Marxists in and beyond Latin America, entitled *Christian Mission and the Utopian Dream*. Though the journal has ceased publication, enquiries could be made via Partnership in Mission, 1564 Edge Hill Road, Abington, Pa. 19001, USA.

The Latin American Theological Fraternity has published a number of papers by various authors on different aspects of liberation theology, notably René Padilla, 'The Kingdom of God and the Church', *Bulletin of the LATF*, 1976, Nos. 1 and 2, and Samuel Escobar 'The Kingdom of God, Eschatology, and Social and Political Ethics in Latin America', *Bulletin of the LATF*, 1975, No. 1.

It is vitally important to realise that liberation theology is not just an interesting extra addition to the collection of world-wide theologies to be added to a theologian's bookshelf. It raises vital questions about the way we do theology, and about the way our own society is organised to benefit or oppress.

Chapter eighteen

Role plays and Simulation games are available from Frontier Youth Trust, 130 City Road, London EC1V 2NJ. *Using simulation games* by Pat Baker is available from the Joint Board of Christian Education of Australia and New Zealand, 147, Collins Street, Melbourne, Victoria 3000, Australia. Games which reproduce the dynamics and lifestyles of Indian villagers are available from SEARCH, 41, 12th Cross, Wilson Gardens, Bangalore 560 027, India. *Monsoon* by John Staley is particularly effective among forty people for three hours. Joe Currie's book, *Learning through doing*, published by AICUF, Sterling Street, Madras 34 gives excellent simulation games and exercises on social awareness, leadership, conflict, change and goal-setting. David Clark in *Basic communities* (SPCK, 1977) gives many lessons in non-directive leadership in Christian community. Discussion questions on simple lifestyles and commitment to the poor based on Ron Sider's *Rich Christians in an age of hunger* (Hodder, 1977) are called *Hard questions for rich Christians* prepared by John Mitchell and Geoff Shearer; this is available from Christian Aid, TEAR Fund or *Third Way*. Many suggestions for simple lifestyles and enjoying simple things free were made by Edith Schaeffer in *Hidden art* (The Norfolk Press, 1971). Art Gish in *Beyond the rat race* (Scotdale Herald Press, 1973) makes many suggestions, as does Beryl Bye in *What about lifestyle* (Paternoster, 1977) and John Taylor in *Enough is enough* (SCM, 1975). John Mitchell in 'Enough is as Good as Feast', *Third Way*, January 1979 suggests how English Christians can calculate basic expenditure in a hungry world.

Brian Wren in *Education for Justice* (SCM, 1977) makes many practical suggestions for helping a group begin to be socially aware. Paulo Freire's works describe the process of making people aware of injustice and their rights, and how they need to act together to achieve them. He put these principles into practice among peasants in Brazil. He was so successful that the Government deported him. See his *Pedagogy of the Oppressed* (Penguin, 1972).

John Gladwin in *God's People in God's World* (IVP, 1979) outlines many practical ideas for Christian social involvement. The Christian Institute of Southern Africa produced a guide for Christian groups who seek to work for change in society.

Two papers on evangelism sparked off the concern for radical discipleship at the Lausanne Congress. They were 'Evangelism and the World' by René Padilla, in the report of the Lausanne Congress on World Evangelisation entitled *Let the Earth Hear His Voice* and edited by J. D. Douglas (World Wide Publications, 1975), pp. 116–133; and 'Evangelism and Man's Search for Freedom, Justice and Fulfilment' by Samuel Escobar, *ibid.*, p. 303–318.

Chapter nineteen

Brian Wren in *Education for justice* (SCM, 1977) has an excellent chapter on 'Learning the realities of power', which explores many of the tactics used by those in power against people trying to bring justice and change. The writings of Martin Luther King are classics on suffering in the course of human justice – see especially *Strength to love* (Collins Fontana, 1974), and *The trumpet of conscience* (Hodder and Stoughton, 1968). John Yoder in *The politics of Jesus* (Eerdmans, 1972) and Martin Hengel in *Victory over violence* (Philadelphia, 1973) discuss Jesus' political strategy of non-violent resistance.

See also the author's *A different dream – non-violent resistance as practical politics* (Grove Booklets on Ethics 12, 1976). Jacque Ellul's study *Violence* (SCM, 1970) has been re-issued (Mowbrays,

1979). He analyses the nature of violence, and argues for non-violent engagement, especially on behalf of the forgotten poor, whose cause does not coincide with the interests of powerful groups.

Two important recent studies are Ron Sider, *Christ and violence* (Lion, 1980), and Andrew Kirk, *Theology encounters revolution* (IVP, 1980) – see especially Appendix B, 'Violence', pp. 141–60. Vinay Samuel's *The meaning and cost of discipleship* (see bibliography to chapter 3) discusses the cost of discipleship for the Church in India.

References

Chapter 1: New perspectives

1 Robert McNamara, Address to UNCTAD III; *in* Duarte Barreto, *India's search for development and social justice 2* (CSA, Bangalore, 1977), p. 48
2 President Julius K. Nyerere, Address to the Maryknoll Sisters' General Chapter, New York 1972; *quoted in* Duarte Barreto, *op. cit.*, p. 50
3 Duarte Barreto, *op. cit.*, p. 43–4
4 Robert Holman, *Poverty: explanations of social deprivation* (Martin Robertson, 1979), p. 43
5 P. Townsend, *The social minority* (Allen Lane 1973), p. 25, *quoted in* Robert Holman, *op. cit.*, p. 43
6 Roy Dorey, 'People without power'; *in* Michael Eastman, *Inside Out* (Falcon, 1976), p. 55 ff.

Chapter 2: What is radical discipleship?

1 The quotation from Rev. David Watson is from the foreword to Ron Sider, *Rich Christians in an age of hunger* (Hodder, 1978). Page references in the text refer to this edition.
2 Peter L. Berger, *A rumour of angels* (Penguin, 1970), p. 32
3 David Clark, *Basic communities* (SPCK, 1977), p. 108–9
4 David and Neta Jackson, *Living together in a world falling apart*; *quoted in* Ron Sider, *op. cit.*, p. 174
5 David Clark, *op. cit.*, p. 212
6 Charles Mellis, *Committed communities: fresh streams of world mission* (William Carey Library, 1976)

7 Michael Eastmann, *Inside out* (Falcon, 1976), p. 19

8 Francois Houtart, *The development project as a social practice of the Church of India* (Lemercinier and Legrand, Louvain 1976)

9 Michael Green, 'Mission and ministry'; *in* Ian Cundy (ed.), *Obeying Christ in a changing world: The people of God* (Collins Fountain, 1977), pp. 75–6

10 The Lausanne Committee sponsored the Willowbank Consultation on Gospel and Culture as part of the follow-up to the Lausanne Congress. The quote is from *The Willow Report: Gospel and Culture* (Lausanne Occasional Papers No 3, 1978) p. 11

11 Thomas Cullinan *The Roots of Social Injustice* (CIIR/CHAS London) p. 4

12 Quoted in *Evangelicals Tomorrow* by John Capon (Collins Fount 1977) p. 77

Chapter 3: The ministry of Jesus

1 Michael Eastman, *Inside out* (Falcon, 1976), p. 20

2 John Yoder, *The Original Revolution* (Herald Press 1971) p. 29

3 In *Frontier Youth Trust Review* (No 6), p. 11

4 Vinay Samuel, *The meaning and cost of discipleship* (BUILD, Bombay, 1981)

5 Richard Cassidy, *Jesus, politics and society* (Orbis, 1978), p. 58–9

6 *Christian witness to the urban poor*: draft statement from the Consultation on World Evangelisation, June 1980, pp. 6–7.

Chapter 4: Jesus is Lord

1 Greg Forster, writing in *Third Way*, 20 April 1978, p. 5

2 C. T. Kurien, *Poverty and development* (CLS, Madras, 1974), p. 17

3 Bruce Kaye, Introduction to Bruce Kaye (ed.), *Obeying Christ in a changing world: 3, The changing world* (Collins, Fountain, 1977), pp. 9–10

4 Martin Luther King Jr., *Strength to love* (Collins Fontana, 1974), p. 92

Chapter 5: The Church – the avant-garde of the New Creation

1 Ron Sider *Rich Christians in an age of hunger* op.cit., p. 73

2 Howard Snyder, *New Wine, New Wineskins* (Marshall Morgan and Scott 1977)

3 Jim Punton 'The Community of shalom' in *Frontier Youth Trust Review* No. 6, p. 13

4 Michael Harper *Let my people grow!* (Hodder and Stoughton 1977)
5 Ian Cundy in 'The Church as community' in Ian Cundy (ed.), *Obeying Christ in a Changing World: 2 The people of God* (Collins Fountain 1977), p. 17
6 World Council of Churches. World Evangelical Fellowship.

Chapter 6: God and society

1 Ron Sider, in Ron Sider and John Stott, *Evangelism, salvation and social justice* (Grove Booklets on Ethics 16, 1976), p. 15
2 Ron Sider, *op. cit.*, p. 19
3 Roger Sainsbury writing in: Michael Eastman (ed.), *Inside out* (Falcon, 1976), p. 66
4 Robert Holman, *Poverty: explanations of social deprivation* (Martin Robertson, 1979), p. 293
5 Vinay Samuel, *The meaning and cost of discipleship* (BUILD, Bombay, 1981)
6 Hendrik Berkhof, *Christ: the meaning of history* (John Knox Press, 1966), p. 174
7 *Ibid.*, p. 88–9
8 *Ibid.*, p. 91

Chapter 7: The Church – the discipleship training centre

1 Sebastian Kappen, *Jesus and freedom* (Orbis, 1977), p. 169
2 Vinay Samuel, *The meaning and cost of discipleship* (BUILD, Bombay, 1981).

Chapter 8: Love and people

1 A. Morgan Derham, 'Springs need no pumps', *Third Way*, 23 February 1978.
2 Donald Hay, *A Christian critique of capitalism* (Grove Booklets on Ethics 5 1975), p. 21

Chapter 9: Poverty, injustice and development

1 *Poverty and development* (TAFTEE-SEARCH programmed course), lesson 15.
2 Vinay Samuel, *The meaning and cost of discipleship* (BUILD, Bombay, 1981)
3 Graham Houghton, *The impoverishment of dependency* (doctoral thesis presented to the University of California, Los Angeles 1980) CLS, Madras, 1983.
4 Vinay Samuel and Charles Corwin, 'Assistance programmes

require partnership', in *Evangelical Review of Theology*, Paternoster Press, April 1980, p. 57

5 T. Scarlett Epstein *South India, Yesterday, Today and Tomorrow* (MacMillan 1973) p. 171

6 Reported in SCAN Spring 1978 p. 2, published by Partnership in Mission

Chapter 10: Communities on the move

1 Chris Wigglesworth, 'The poorest of the poor', *Third Way*, 9 February 1978.

Chapter 11: Teaching by evangelism

1 Kevin Shergold writing in: Michael Eastman (ed.), *Inside out* (Falcon, 1976), p. 28

2 Statement issued by the Theological Work Group of the Nationwide Initiative in Evangelism including Roman Catholics and Evangelicals in Evangelism, June 1980.

3 Roy Dorey writing in: Michael Eastman, *op. cit.*, p. 59

4 Said in personal conversation with the author.

5 A. Morgan Derham, 'Springs need no pumps', *Third Way*, 23 February 1978.

Chapter 12: Teaching by calling to repentance

1 Rene Padilla, 'Evangelism and the world', in: J. D. Douglas (ed.), *Let the earth hear his voice* (World-wide Publications, 1975), p. 29

2 Ron Sider, *Rich Christians in an age of hunger* op.cit., p. 123–4

Chapter 13: Counselling new Christians

1 Michael Harper, 'Christian maturing', in: John Stott (ed.), *Obeying Christ in a changing world: 1, The Lord Christ* (Collins Fountain, 1977), p. 146

2 *The Nottingham statement: the official statement of the second National Evangelical Anglican Congress held in April 1977* (Falcon, 1977), p. 30

Chapter 14: The whole community teaches discipleship

1 Peter Lee, *Equipping God's people* (Grove Booklets on Ministry and Worship, 45)

Chapter 15: How to do theology

1 Charles Kraft, *Christianity in culture* (Orbis, 1979)

Chapter 17: Commitment and action

1 Ron McMullen, 'Christian youth work in relation to the community', *Frontier Youth Trust Review* (6)

Chapter 18: Action and reflection

1 John Root, writing in *Third Way*, May 1979, p. 4
2 Ron Sider, *Rich Christians in an age of hunger* (Hodder, 1979), pp. 152–4
3 *Hard Questions for Rich Christians* Supplement to *Third Way* August 1979 published by the Thirty Press
4 Kevin Shergold, 'Suburban realities': in Michael Eastmann, *Inside out* (Falcon, 1976), p. 33. The quote from T. R. Batten which follows is quoted by Kevin Shergold in the chapter cited.

Chapter 19: The cost of radical discipleship

1 Martin Luther King Jr., *Why we can't wait* (Signet Books, New York, 1974), p. 84 ff.

Updated Bibliography

Since the first edition was published eighteen months ago, a number of books have appeared which develop further themes of Radical Discipleship. For reasons of space I will merely note their details. Most authors will be familiar from the earlier bibliographical material:

Evangelism and Social Responsibility – An Evangelical Statement (The Grand Rapids Report) pub. Lausanne Committee and World Evangelical Fellowship, Paternoster Press, 1982. Orlando Costas *Christ Outside the Gate: Mission Beyond Christendom* (Orbis, 1982). Donald Hay *A Christian Critique of Socialism* (Grove Books, 1982). Michael Paget-Wilkes *Poverty, Revolution and the Church* (Paternoster, 1981). John Stanley *People in Development, A Training Manual for Groups* (Search, Bangalore, 1982). Vinay Samuel and Chris Sugden *Current Trends in Theology, A Third World Guide; Christian Mission in the Eighties: A Third World Perspective; Evangelism and the Poor: A Third World Study Guide* published by Partnership in Mission Asia, P.O. Box 544, Bangalore 560005, India. See also *Sharing Jesus in the Two Thirds World* (papers from the first conference of evangelical mission theologians from the Two Thirds World) edited by Vinay Samuel and Chris Sugden, Partnership in Mission Asia 1983, also available from Asian Trading Corporation, 150 Brigade Road, Bangalore 560025. Stephen Travis *I Believe in the Second Coming of Jesus* (Hodder and Stoughton 1982). Jim Wallis *The Call to Conversion* (Lion 1982). *Unemployment Study Pack for Groups* 'A World that Doesn't Care' by Aslancrafts Educational Unit, 15 Queen Square, Leeds 2.